THE BOOK OF REVELATION

THE BOO

PHILADELPH

# of REVELATION

BY ARNE UNJHEM

FRANK W. KLOS·EDITOR

LAJOS SZALAY·ARTIST

THERAN CHURCH PRESS

LCA School of Religion Series

This pupil's book is accompanied by a teacher's guide, *The Book of Revelation* (SR A).

Printed in the United States of America
7289D78   19-429

Preface

THE last book of the Bible is unknown and somewhat mysterious for many modern Christians. Those who venture beyond the end of the third chapter soon feel lost amid a profusion of weird symbols and uncanny events that seem completely unrelated to the world of daily experience. A few paragraphs here and there may stand out as meaningful and inspiring, but the book as a whole seems beyond comprehension.

This situation is not helped by the fact that some groups within the Christian church have treated Revelation as a book of oracles that enables them to predict many future events, including the end of the world. On the basis of such predictions, there have been those who have withdrawn from participation in everyday life and have even gathered to await the "coming of Christ" on specific dates forecast by their leaders.

It is not strange, therefore, that many a modern Christian tends to associate Revelation with extremism and emotionalism. Yet he is also aware that Revelation is part of the Bible and must be important. He is quite convinced that someday he really ought to take time to find out what Revelation can mean to him. And he feels, too, that he will need some assistance in his task.

The Book of Revelation

You need no special qualifications to study Revelation effectively except a willingness to spend some time and effort in reading and thinking. If you are willing to do this, this book will offer assistance as you become involved in a serious exploration of Revelation. However, this is not a traditional chapter-by-chapter, verse-by-verse commentary. There are many good commentaries readily available which can be very useful after you have become somewhat familiar with Revelation as a whole. Rather, this book is designed as a guide to show you how to discover for yourself the many treasures that Revelation contains.

No claims are made about infallibility in any of the suggestions offered in this book. Keep an open mind as you study them. The main purpose of this book is to let Revelation speak to you and to all modern Christians as the Word of God.

Contents

	PREFACE	5
1.	ISLAND PROPHET	11
2.	ON BEING A HUMAN BEING	19
3.	LOOKING TOWARD THE FUTURE	27
4.	READING REVELATION	36
5.	THE STRUCTURE OF REVELATION	44
6.	THE CENTER OF REVELATION	54
7.	THE CHURCH IN THE WORLD	63
8.	THE VISIONS OF THE FUTURE	72
9.	THE SYMBOLISM OF REVELATION	82
10.	THE MESSAGE OF THE SYMBOLS	90
11.	THE PATTERN OF THE VISIONS	100
12.	THE SOCIETY OF MEN	112
13.	THE NEW COMMUNITY	122
14.	HISTORY AND THE NEW COMMUNITY	133

This is a Revelation from Jesus Christ, which God gave him so that he might show his servants what must very soon take place. He made it known by sending his angel to his servant John, who is the witness of all that he saw—the message of God, and the testimony of Jesus Christ.

Happy is the man who reads this prophecy and happy are those who hear it read and pay attention to its message; for the time is near.

John, to the seven Churches in Asia:

Grace and peace be to you from him who is and who was and who is coming, from the seven Spirits before his throne, and from Jesus Christ the faithful witness, firstborn of the dead, and ruler of kings upon earth. To him who loves us and has set us free from our sins through his own blood, who has made us a kingdom of priests to his God and Father, to him be glory and power for timeless ages, amen!

See, he is coming in the clouds and every eye shall see him, even those who pierced him, and his coming will mean bitter sorrow to every tribe upon the earth. So let it be!

"I am Alpha and Omega," says the Lord God, "who is and who was and who is coming, the Almighty."

REVELATION 1:1–8
J. B. Phillips translation

1 · Island Prophet

THE island of Patmos lies in the Aegean Sea, about thirty miles off the western coast of modern Turkey, opposite the region called the province of Asia in New Testament times. A visitor coming across the water toward the island will first notice a wall of white cliffs rising some eight hundred feet above the sea. When he lands he will find that most of the island is rocky and bare, providing a frugal living for only a small number of people.

The limited resources and uninviting physical aspect of Patmos may have been the reason the island remained untouched by the Greek civilization that flourished on other islands in the Aegean Sea. The only fame that Patmos acquired came later, in the Roman Empire, when the island was used as a penal colony for political prisoners. These prisoners were forced to work in the stone quarries on the island, often until they died from starvation and hard labor.

Who Was John?

Among those who were brought to the island under these circumstances was the author of the last book of the Bible. The name of this man was John (Revelation 1:9), but not much else is known about him now. The name has led many to think that he was John the son of Zebedee, one of the twelve disciples of Christ. A very old tradition maintains that this John spent the last years of his life in Ephesus, the capital of the province of Asia. If this is true, it is not impossible that he, being the leader of the churches in this region, could have been sentenced to imprisonment on Patmos and there experienced the visions that are recorded in Revelation. But other traditions, just as venerable, seem to deny this. John was a rather common name; and there is nothing in Revelation itself to help modern scholars positively identify the author.

Although the identity of the author remains unknown, this does not mean that he was a person of no importance. The fact that the Roman authorities in the province of Asia had made him a target in their warfare against the churches in this area suggests that he was a prominent church leader. As we read his book we notice also that he was well acquainted with many of the congregations in the region and in turn expected them to recognize his name and position. Above all, we can discern in his book a great concern for the spiritual welfare of these congregations. He also had an absorbing interest in the future of the kingdom of God on earth: he looked to the time when "The kingdom of the world has become the kingdom of our Lord and of his Christ . . ." (11:15). These are qualities that make a spiritual leader in any age.

Emperor Worship

The external circumstances that brought John to Patmos and set the stage for the visions recorded in Revelation are somewhat better known than John himself. Bible scholars agree that John's imprisonment took place near the end of the reign of Emperor Domitian (A.D. 81–96), at a time when the issue of emperor worship was becoming a source of open conflict between the Christian church and Roman authorities in the province of Asia.

The practice of emperor worship had begun during the reign of Augustus (31 B.C.–A.D. 14), and it may have been tolerated or encouraged by most of the emperors who came after him. In the beginning it was mainly a political device, serving much the same purpose as our pledge of allegiance to the flag, in this way binding together the many incongruous elements in the vast Roman Empire in a common ceremonial expression of loyalty to Rome. The rite, at which the average citizen remained just a spectator, was usually performed by local public officials once a year. But under Domitian this changed. He was a vain and despotic emperor who demanded that all his underlings should address him as "Our Lord and God," and he decreed that every citizen should have an active part in the emperor worship.

The emperor cult could be nothing but an abomination to both Christians and Jews. To put a finite human being in the place that belongs to God is idolatry and a direct violation of the First Commandment. The decree was all the more sinister because Domitian himself was a shocking example of the moral corruption that was wasting the Roman Empire. To worship such a man as God would be nothing less than total surrender to the forces of evil and a betrayal of Christ.

The Jews had consistently opposed emperor worship as a violation of their religious convictions; generally Roman authorities excused them from participation. If the Christian church had remained a small sect within the framework of Judaism, it might well have enjoyed the same privilege. But by the end of the first century, Christianity had already gone far beyond the Judaic environment in which it was born and had become a religion of all races. In most churches there were more people from Gentile than Jewish backgrounds, and the Roman authorities ruled that all Christians were obliged to take part in emperor worship. It seems clear that the authorities in the province of Asia, for political reasons, were especially anxious to enforce the decree.

Persecution

The persecution of Christians under Domitian was not the first experience of such difficulties for the church. During the

13

reign of Nero (A.D. 54–68) many believers had suffered martyrdom in the western part of the empire. Nero may have acted mainly from political motives when he attacked the church at that time, but for the Christians the experience was a warning of their alien and precarious position in the Roman state. Nero committed suicide in A.D. 68, but a rumor spread that he would soon rise again from the dead and lead the forces of evil in an all-out attack on the Christian church. His name thus became the symbol for the threat of secular power organized in opposition to the kingdom of God.

The Christians living under these uncertain conditions at the end of the first century could find little encouragement as they contemplated the structure and aims of political power. The secular state seemed to be on the side of evil, the kingdom of man arrayed against the kingdom of God. The future looked dark, and Domitian's program of enforced emperor worship could only be interpreted as a prelude to the final, head-on conflict between good and evil.

John had doubtless resisted by word and example the effort to make Christian believers worship the emperor. His banishment to Patmos served the double purpose of removing him from his position of leadership and notifying others of what would happen if they continued their resistance to emperor worship. The concentration camp to which John was sent also had another purpose: to "reeducate" its inmates by the harsh methods of enforced isolation, hard work, and near-starvation diet. Nothing could please the Roman authorities more than to be able to send John back to the mainland someday with his spirit broken and his effectiveness as a leader of the churches reduced to nothing.

A Time of Visions

A penal colony on a barren island seems like an impossible background for visions about the future of the kingdom of God. But this is not the first, nor is it the last time that something of great significance appeared in an unlikely setting. God often reveals himself where human resources are at their

REVELATION 1:13–16

lowest ebb. One can easily picture John's sense of isolation and his concern about the churches he had been forced to leave. On a clear day he could see the mountains of the mainland rising above the sea, and in his mind's eye he could see the well-known towns with their Christian congregations. It is not difficult to imagine that this sense of isolation and concern was especially keen on the Lord's Day, the day of worship, when John would ordinarily have been breaking the bread with his fellow believers.

On such a Lord's Day it happened: as John "was in the Spirit" (1:10) he heard a voice and received the command to write down the visions that he was about to see. The setting of Revelation in a Lord's-Day experience is important. John's orientation to the gospel of Christ is in terms of the Christian community, the church. Present-day visitors to Patmos are shown a cave that is said to be the very spot where John had his visions. Like most other places that are identified with particular events recorded in the New Testament, this one is probably nothing more than a guess hallowed by tradition.

Inspiration

The exact place where John experienced his visions is not really important, but the student of Revelation cannot help being curious about the nature of his experience. Did John go into some kind of trance and in this state write down the words of Revelation as we have them now in the Greek version of the New Testament? And did this happen all in the course of one day?

Some people like to think that the whole Bible was produced in some such way: the authors, being only passive instruments completely possessed by God's Spirit, hardly knew what they were doing while they were writing. This is what some people understand by "inspiration," and they like this theory because it seems to be an insurance against human errors creeping into divine revelation.

But this understanding of the way in which God reveals himself to man is open to serious question. In the first place, if this is how God wanted to reveal his Word, why did he bother with human writers at all? Why did he not create the books already written? Furthermore, this understanding of inspiration is really a pagan idea that is out of harmony with the biblical understanding of how God works. For instance, the ancient Greeks had a famous oracle at Delphi where messages said to be of divine origin could be received. In virtually all religions there is some form of divination deeply involved in magic and superstitions. To reduce the biblical understanding of revelation to this is, to reverse an old saying, like turning a silk purse into a sow's ear.

The chief emphasis in the biblical understanding of man's relationship to God is that this relationship can never be reduced to an impersonal and automatic level, and this applies to revelation as well as to everything else. This means that we respond to God's self-disclosure with all our faculties intact, "with all your heart, and with all your soul, and with all your mind." The person who receives a revelation from God does not cease to function as the person he is: his knowledge, his feelings, his social and cultural background, his particular situation all become a vital part of the revelatory experience.

In the Spirit

What, then, makes a revelatory experience different from any other experience? John's statement that he "was in the Spirit" points to this difference. It suggests a special point of view, not an ordinary human viewpoint. The word "ecstasy" is often used to describe this special point of view. In spite of the fact that in popular usage this word may suggest great emotional upheaval or even some kind of trance, this is not the meaning it has in theology. The word "ecstasy" comes from two Greek words, *ek* (meaning "out") and *histanai* (meaning "to stand"). Together they give the meaning of "standing out" or "standing apart from." To be in ecstasy or "in the Spirit" means to step aside or step out from one's ordinary position and see things from a different perspective. It means to be,

17

literally, "out of your mind," outside or removed from or above your normal, everyday self.

The ecstatic experience is not something that man can cultivate in himself. As John makes clear in several connections, all a man can do here is respond to an invitation (4:1). But when a man does respond to such an invitation, he does not leave himself behind. And when he reports on what is revealed to him in his ecstasy, he uses the means that are within his reach. Who and where he is are apparent in his work. For instance, the royal background of the prophet Isaiah shows clearly in his writings, just as the rural environment of the prophet Amos is apparent in what he wrote.

The fundamental fact about John and his visions is that he had an ecstatic experience, in which "God gave him to show to his servants what must soon take place" (1:1). How this got to be written down, how long it took to do this writing, and what means John used to express the revelation he received ought not be confused with the fundamental fact of this revelation. It is, of course, important to understand John's method of expressing himself if we want to understand the meaning of his revelation. It is important, too, to understand as much as possible of the background from which John delivered his message. Indeed, it is impossible to understand most of John's symbolism except in relation to this background. Finally, it is important to understand the kind of problems to which John's message was addressed. It is a common human failing to want answers before the questions are fully understood. Much of the confusion and misunderstanding that has developed in connection with the Book of Revelation may be due to the fact that people have looked for answers to the wrong kind of questions.

Your study of Revelation must therefore begin on the island of Patmos where John was; and it must arise out of the same concern which filled John as he searched for signs of what the future would bring to those who had committed their lives to Christ.

2 · On Being a Human Being

AMONG the many questions that are dealt with as you read Revelation is "What does it mean to be a human being?"

There are a great many answers to this question, all of them pointing to some part of the truth. As the Greeks were fond of saying, man is a rational being, capable of using his mind for great things. But man is also a child of nature, subject to the process of change and decay. He often acts contrary to his own best judgments, driven by passions and desires that he can barely understand. He is also a social being, dependent on others for the needs of his own existence; yet he often finds himself in conflict with his fellow human beings. He also feels a need to believe in something higher than himself.

One of the most significant answers emphasizes the historical character of human existence: We always live on the boundary between a receding past and a future that may be both promising and threatening.

There is, first of all, the history of each person—the irreversible process of growing up, then growing older, and lastly growing old. As a nation we are great admirers of youth, both in the sense of physical vigor and the kind of limitless opportunity that being young seems to imply. We tend to resent the signs of aging, as though they represent some personal failure and defeat.

Problems

Our admiration of youth and resentment of old age may result from the emphasis in our culture on achievement: the tasks to be done, the knowledge to be gained, the new frontiers to be mastered. Anything that represents flagging energy and waning ambitions obviously is out of step with this restless drive. But does the problem go deeper than that?

Consider, for example, the limited scope of human life. In childhood the life that lies ahead seems like an endless expanse with unlimited opportunities about which one can dream and hope while waiting for the slow passage of time. But as one grows older the years pass by more quickly and the range of opportunities becomes more narrow. There comes the crisis of middle age when, whether we want to or not, we must face the fact that many of the dreams of our childhood and youth will never be fulfilled. And in old age we have to come to terms with the fact that, for better or worse, we have spent our life—irrevocably and absolutely.

Answers

Man cannot avoid the problems of living within a limited historical scope, of beginning to die as soon as one is born. Ancient man and modern man are quite alike in this respect even if the outward circumstances of their existence have little in common. And how does a person, ancient or modern, come to terms with these facts of his existence?

Some people, both now and in the past, have suggested that stoic resignation is the answer. We must learn to accept the inevitable even if our whole being rebels against it. But there are just as many people who have been fascinated by the possibility of overcoming the limitations of age and decay. The old dream of finding the "fountain of youth" and the modern hope that medical science will learn to cope with physical and mental deterioration are snips of the same cloth in this respect. But is living forever in this world—even in good physical health and with unimpeded mental powers—really what man wants? Does not the old fable about the Wandering Jew whose perpetual existence on earth was a punishment suggest a profound truth? Is not the possibility of being part of a larger history, a history that extends beyond the life of an individual here on earth, much more promising?

A Link in the Chain

All of us are part of a larger history in the sense that we have parents and ancestors and may in turn become parents and ancestors of future generations. We are enjoying the benefits and suffering the consequences of what earlier generations have done, and we will by our own actions contribute to the joys and sorrows of future generations. Each person is only a link in a long historical chain of which we can see neither the beginning nor the end.

In general, we are not tremendously conscious of this larger history to which we belong. We tend to look upon the past as ages of ignorance and error; and while we often speak enthusiastically about the great future, we use our resources and despoil our environment as though we have no concern about the needs and enjoyments of future generations. What is the reason for this reluctance to come to terms with our role as historical beings?

Progress

Doubtless one reason is that we have been so completely committed to what we call "progress" that anything that shows the sign of belonging to the past is automatically regarded as inferior. Advertisers are forever trying to sell us a "completely new" product. Whatever is latest is always presented as the best. Not to be "with it," whether this has to do with the most recent art, dress styles, home furnishings, or car models, is for many people a fate worse than death. But is there a deeper problem here, too?

REVELATION 5:6–7

For instance, what is the nature of this fascination with progress? Why are we enamored by everything that appears to be new? Do not these attitudes reflect a sense of disappointment with what has been achieved so far and a restless search for something better?

From time to time social and political reform movements have appeared, often inspired by noble ideals and high hopes. As we look over the known history of the human race, we can certainly perceive some progress: there is obviously some difference between modern society and the tyrannical rules of ancient potentates. But it is also obvious that no society is safe from corruption. The Utopian hope that some innovation—a new political system, reorganization of the economic structure, the scientific manipulation of all human problems, or the organization of a community of selected members—seems, in our day and age, strangely unrealistic. Yet we keep dreaming.

A Better Future

Hoping for a better future is not something that only modern man experiences. The Old Testament prophets spoke often about such a hope. The Greek philosopher Plato drew a blueprint of an ideal society, ruled by a philosopher-king, in which all citizens would find complete satisfaction and happiness. Many other such plans have been prepared from time to time. The chief attraction of Marxist philosophy for many underdeveloped nations is its promise of a better future. Without a doubt, a better future is a universal human desire. But are there any real grounds for such a hope?

Many thinkers have suggested that the best way to find an answer to this question is to study the course of history. But others have insisted that historical developments are largely meaningless series of events, showing little direction or purpose. And a sense of meaning and purpose seems to be what people crave. With a sense of meaning and purpose, hardships can be endured and difficulties overcome. Without it, we are left with a void that the pursuit of novelty for its own sake can never fill.

THE BOOK OF REVELATION
John the Visionary

In the Book of Revelation, John attempts to say something specific about what it means to be a human being caught in a historical process. As he deals with time and eternity, with faith and history, he fulfills his role as a prophet of God. A prophet or a visionary is sometimes described as a person who has his feet on the ground and his head in the clouds. He is also described as someone who is seeing the invisible or discerning meanings that escape the average person.

A genuine prophet is himself caught in the dilemmas and predicaments with which his prophecy is concerned. The Isaiah who was chosen as God's messenger to his people was a man who knew from personal experience about the menace of "unclean lips" (Isaiah 6:5–9). And the visions recorded in the Book of Revelation came to a man who had been caught in the conflict that the visions were about.

If this is true of prophets, it is also true of those who would learn to understand what the prophets speak about. So long as we remain detached and unconcerned, the words of the prophets will make no sense to us. We must be willing to make the troubles of the world our own concerns if we wish to know the meaning of prophecy.

But we must also beware when we do this: It is possible to become crushed by the world's problems, to know only defeat or despair, or else cynicism, in our evaluation of the possibilities that lie ahead. What makes a prophet able to endure the discouraging facts of life and still sound a note of hope in his message to the world?

One reason is that the prophet does not go by outward manifestations only, but looks for inner meaning. He does not run away from whatever is harsh and unpleasant, but on the other hand he is not a pessimist. He is committed to the belief that regardless of what the immediate evidence seems to suggest, the world and its affairs are in the hands of God and everything will eventually work out according to his design.

The prophet has reached a point where his life is surrendered to God. This means that obedience to the will of

God becomes the leading motive of his life, even when such obedience entails an extra burden of suffering and sorrow. And all this also applies to those who would understand the message of the prophet.

Prophetic Viewpoint

The prophet's viewpoint is far removed from the superficial optimism of those who claim that "God's in His heaven —All's right with the world!" If there is one thing that the prophet is sure of, it is that all is *not* right with the world. But he also knows that God is not in some remote heaven, removed from the problems of the world. God's active presence in the world is the central insight of all prophecy.

The prophet is always a child of his own times, standing in an immediate relation to the troubles that afflict himself and his contemporaries. He speaks their language, shares their limitations, participates in their style of living, reflects in his own person the circumstances and peculiarities that give a distinct character to people in a given time and place.

What, then, makes us recognize a spiritual kinship with prophets of other ages? Is there something that transcends cultural differences and speaks to our common humanity? The Roman Empire that loomed so large in John's visions of the future may be to us just a bit of poorly remembered history; and Revelation's images of mounted warriors, beasts, sounding trumpets, and women in purple robes are like pictures in an old book of fairy tales. What can be the connection between these and our world of fast cars, scientific methods, and global culture?

Artistic Language

Obviously, any attempt to interpret John's visions in a literal sense will make them completely irrelevant to our way of life. But suppose we are willing to let our imagination have some freedom here and grant, too, that God's resources in addressing himself to humanity may be more varied and ingenious than sober-minded theologians have tended to think?

We can read Revelation as a picturesque account of what is essentially a spiritual struggle, an "invisible" process in our own world, just as revelant to American suburbia and the metropolitan scene as it was to the seven small towns in Asia Minor where the message was first read.

What do we discover, then, when we agree to read Revelation as a prophecy expressed by means of artistic rather than factual language? We can hardly avoid recognizing two of John's questions that are very much our own: What is the meaning of our personal history in this world? and, What can we expect from our participation in the ongoing historical process to which we belong? And from these, other questions arise and are dealt with. What is the answer to the decay and death that threaten human existence? How do we cope with the sense of dissatisfaction that attends our experiences here on earth? What is the nature of the corruption that seems to afflict all our attempts to make this life a meaningful experience? What are the grounds for the hope that life will not be just a futile pursuit of novelty, but lead to genuine renewal for both individuals and communities? What are the conditions under which hostility and hate give way to real fellowship with others?

3 · Looking Toward the Future

CONCERN about the future and what the future will bring, therefore, did not begin with John on Patmos, nor is it limited to people who, like him, are confronted with special problems and difficulties. As some Greek philosophers observed long ago, we are always in the process of becoming. Each moment of life is a step into the unknown, into a future that is at least partly hidden. Each day presents new possibilities and hazards that are not always easy to anticipate. And over all our experience is the haunting awareness that the life we now enjoy must someday end and that most of the things we cherish are temporary and finite.

Predictions

It is not surprising, therefore, that since the dawn of history man has tried to look into the future, both to predict events and to find guidance in choosing the best possible courses of action. In all known cultures, we can find evidence of the practice of divination—the art of foretelling future events by means of special techniques such as studying the entrails of animals, the flight of birds, the pattern formed by a bunch of sticks thrown on the ground.

27

Dreams were often thought to reveal the future, and it is still possible to buy books that will offer interpretations of dreams in this way. Several thousand years ago, Babylonian magi developed the theory that human fate is intimately connected with the constellation of stars at the time of birth of each individual. Astrological charts have been prepared all over the world ever since, and Americans spend many millions of dollars each year on them.

In all ages there have been people who seemed to have some special power or ability to look into the future, and they have always been regarded with awe and respect by those who believed in their powers. In all religions there have been seers and prophets who would speak about things that had not yet happened as though they had already seen the outcome.

It may seem odd to mention modern science in this connection, but in it can be seen the same concern with the future. It is the ideal of all science to learn the nature of things so well that future behavior can be predicted with accuracy. Of course, methods of modern science differ vastly from the techniques of astrologers and soothsayers, but in one sense the aim is the same.

Purpose

We may feel confident that we have nothing to do with the superstitious ideas that have beclouded the minds of people in past ages, but there is still the matter of the unknown future. And as we think about the past and the future from our narrow vantage point in the present, we cannot avoid asking whether there is some clear purpose to our existence here on earth. It is true that each of us has his own purposes that give some sense of direction to his life. We also can have purposes in common with other members of the community to which we belong, and we work together with them for the realization of these purposes.

But the question of the purpose of existence goes beyond all this, to whether there is some universal purpose that transcends our own life and hence bestows some larger meaning upon our limited and temporary existence. If this were the case, then could not one expect to see some manifestation of this purpose in the pattern of events that take shape as time moves on from the past into the future? If we can discover such a universal purpose it will help us better understand our own role in what may otherwise seem a meaningless flow of events.

Theories of History

The possibility of discovering some pattern and purpose in historical developments has always fascinated men. The results of their thinking have been expressed in many different ways, from crude mythologies to highly sophisticated philosophies of history. Most of these theories fall into one of these three classes: circular, evolutionary, or dialectic interpretations of history.

In the circular theory of history, the flow of events is regarded as an infinite series of cycles in which history repeats itself again and again. What is happening now has happened many times before and will happen again. This view usually goes hand in hand with determinism—the belief that there is no genuine freedom for man, that he is under the dominion of powers that shape his life and destiny with ruthless indifference. The best man can do is accept his fate stoically and not dissipate his life in senseless rebellion against the inevitable. Very often the prevailing mood in this view is one of profound pessimism.

The evolutionary view of history is one which appeals to modern people because it seems to be both scientific and optimistic. According to this view there is a steady movement toward higher and better forms of existence; and man himself may take an active part in accelerating this movement through education, scientific research and planning, and democratic political and social living. There is seldom a clearly conceived goal toward which history is moving in this view. The general direction is toward "progress," and some interpreters of this view maintain that there is no limit to the possibilities of progress. But world wars and cold wars and racial tensions and all the other ailments of modern society tend to challenge faith in unlimited progress.

In the dialectic view of history, the idea of conflict is predominant. Some ancient versions of this view involved a struggle between divine and demonic beings carried on in the world, manifesting itself in historical developments. In the Marxist adaptation of this view the supernatural elements have disappeared and the conflict is interpreted in strictly materialistic terms. But there are still others, neither primitive nor Marxist, who hold that historical happenings reveal a fundamental tension between opposing elements. Any progress here is the result of the seesaw movement of opposing forces, and the struggle is endless.

The Bible and History

We need not read very far in the Bible to realize that here, too, there is a great concern with the meaning of history and the implications of this meaning for individual life. The writers of the Old Testament were not merely recording the events of the past. They were trying to show how the origin and development of the Jewish nation fitted into a grand plan for the whole world. The calling of Abraham as the founder of the Jewish nation was not just a matter of national interest but something that would make "all the nations of the earth bless themselves" (Genesis 22:18).

Prominent in this outlook was the view of the Jewish nation as a chosen people. There were many privileges and blessings attached to this position, and there were many times when pride got the upper hand as the Jews contemplated their own position in relation to what they scornfully called "the Gentiles." But the great Jewish leaders were always keenly aware of the responsibility that went with the status as a chosen people. They tried to show that the successes or failures of the Jewish nation were closely related to the way in which the people accepted or rejected their responsibility as a chosen people with a mission.

REVELATION 6:1–8

Testing

The grand vision of a divine purpose for the Jewish nation and the whole world was put to a severe test in the sixth century B.C. when the destruction of Jerusalem and the deportation of the Jews to Babylonia seemed to put an end to the nation's career as a chosen people. The prophets who lived before the Babylonian exile had warned that such a disaster was inevitable if the people of Israel continued to ignore the terms and responsibilities of their calling. But often these prophets had been regarded as alarmists.

In Babylon, the Jews had a chance to reflect on the price of their disobedience. With Jerusalem in ruins, the great temple of Solomon razed, and the people of Israel enduring serfdom more than 500 miles from their homeland, was not every reason for hope gone? There were prophets among the people in Babylonia, too, and they spoke of the need for repentance and rededication. But would this be enough? Those who were aware of the tangled political situation in the Near East could easily see that the fate of the Jewish nation was deeply involved in the struggle for power among the would-be master nations. The leaders of these competing nations seemed to know little and care less about God and his plan for the world, and for them the Jewish people and the land they had been given were nothing more than pawns. The future seemed to belong to those who could amass the greatest military power and use it most effectively. Could the simple faith of Abraham, a trusting fellowship with God in a rustic environment, mean anything in the turmoil of international power politics?

These were questions that could not be ignored by those who took seriously the covenant idea. The fact that the Jews were eventually permitted to return to their homeland by no means solved all the problems, for the centuries that followed the return were marked by strife as the supremacy in the Mediterranean passed from the Persians to the Macedonians and then to the Romans. During this period the Jews were ruled by Gentiles and suffered untold indignities in their own homeland. The memory of the great days under David and

Solomon only accentuated their misery. There were some people, both leaders of the Jews and others, who advocated a "realistic" adjustment to the political facts of the day—which meant cooperation with the alien rulers for the sake of a chance to live as well as possible, even at the price of compromise in matters of faith and morality. But in every generation there were those who kept alive the vision of a chosen people and a divine purpose for the world.

For many who dreamed of the restoration of the people of Israel, this hope expressed itself in very concrete terms. They expected that someday God would raise up another man like King David who would muster the nation, drive out the foreign occupants, and reestablish Israel as an independent and prosperous nation. If the military resources of the Jews seemed puny in comparison with the power of the Roman legions, God would fight with them as he had done when Gideon defeated a mighty army with just a handful of men. The only thing required was the repentance and rededication of the whole nation, and for this was needed a great prophet like Elijah, who had once led a movement to renounce foreign idols and restore faith in God.

Apocalyptic Thinking

But this kind of simple religious nationalism was not the only viewpoint among those who hoped for a divine intervention in human affairs. In the centuries following the Babylonian captivity, there developed among the Jews a distinctly different outlook which is commonly described by the word "apocalyptic." This word comes from two Greek words, the preposition *apo* (meaning "away from" or "off") and the verb *kalyptein* (meaning "to cover"). The basic meaning of this word is thus "to uncover" or "to reveal" what is not apparent to the naked eye.

Bible scholars agree that the early development of apocalyptic thinking among the Jews may have been the result of Jewish contact with Babylonian culture, especially Zoroastrian religion. The use of numerology, astrological symbols, and other such devices in Jewish apocalyptic writings seems to confirm this. But it is also clear that with the passing of time the apocalyptic outlook became an integral part of the religious life of the Jews. The Dead Sea Scrolls have shown that in the centuries just before and after the birth of Christ the apocalyptic view was a strong element in Jewish thought, inspiring not only such radical groups as the Essenes but much popular piety.

According to the apocalyptic view there is a constant struggle in this world. But the struggle is nothing so simple as a war between Jewish nationalists and the legions of Rome, or any other such conflict between particular nations at a given time. A look behind the scenes will reveal that the universe is a gigantic battleground for divine and satanic forces. No one can remain neutral in this struggle, and it seems that the majority of the world's people are on the evil side. While the struggle lasts, the righteous minority can do little more than suffer patiently the indignities and cruelties to which they are subjected. But they can rest assured that the ultimate victory belongs to God and those who remain faithful to him. This victory will inaugurate the "new age" or the "new world" in which those who have remained loyal will enjoy perfect happiness forever in fellowship with God. The world will be changed because God is alive and working for men.

It is quite obvious that John, the author of Revelation, was well acquainted with the apocalyptic tradition and its literature. Many of his symbols are borrowed from Ezekiel and Daniel, the Old Testament writers who express most clearly the apocalyptic viewpoint. There is no way of knowing how familiar his original readers were with this tradition, but their own circumstances as members of the new people of God, the Christian church, made them quite ready to understand and appreciate John's message. The concept of two kingdoms in conflict described their situation as they watched the Roman state turning against them. This was not a matter of academic speculation but something that touched their very existence.

A Story of Conflict

As we compare the message of Revelation with earlier Jewish apocalyptic writings we notice one important new note. In John's book Christ stands out as the key figure. He is clearly the master of the situation and also the leader of the forces that will eventually overcome evil. The victory has already been won by him in his death and resurrection, and all that remains to be done is to make this victory real in the world. The outcome is assured, and for the Christian the only problem is to remain faithful and endure patiently until "the former things have passed away" (Revelation 21:4).

For us in the twentieth century, this apocalyptic viewpoint may seem strange and even incredible. We may note a certain general similarity between this view and what was described above as the dialectic interpretation of history. But even if we are willing to give an open-minded hearing to this interpretation, the form in which it is presented in Revelation seems as antiquated as the armaments with which the Roman legions fought their battles. Whether we will be able to penetrate beneath this form and perceive the enduring message of Revelation depends largely on our willingness to read the book as it was written by the author—as a dramatic, symbolic presentation of the conflict between good and evil in the world.

The issues with which Revelation deals—the meaning of existence, the importance of the witnessing Christian fellowship, the possibilities of the future, and the ultimate goal toward which all things point—are by no means antiquated. Modern man has as many reasons for being concerned about these problems as did man in the first century. He needs only to remember that men now have in their hands the means for laying waste the earth in a conflagration just as devastating as anything envisioned by John. And he hardly needs to be reminded that evil is still a powerful force in all his day-to-day relationships.

4 · Reading Revelation

FTEN our copies of the Bible are printed on special paper with a special binding that sets it apart from other books. This unique physical appearance tends to make us forget that this "book" is not really one book but a whole library, a series of books written in the course of many centuries by many different people and in three different languages—Hebrew, Aramaic, and Greek.

Leafing through the pages of the Bible, we also come upon many different styles of writing, such as poetry, epic narrative, biography, romance, drama, history, and essay. The Word coming from God to man can find expression in all the means through which people try to communicate ideas.

Transmitting Facts

As people living in a culture in which science and its disciplined search for facts plays such a large role, we are generally prejudiced in favor of one style of writing—the terse, factual, objective report. We tend to regard this as more "true" and "credible" than literary forms that appeal to the imagination and the feelings. We will listen respectfully to the astronomer's factual account of what really happens when "the sun sets in the west," but we may easily dismiss the poet's account of the same event as a subjective and irrelevant dream. But what is a "fact"? If we want to know the physical reasons why the sun seems to disappear below the horizon every night, we will do well to listen carefully to the astronomer. But is the human response to the grand display of colors in the western sky, as only a poet or an artist can describe it, any less factual than what the astronomer talks about? Actually, if we consider the whole range of human experience, the language of the artist is as important as the language of the scientist. Feelings and imagination are as much the result of God's creative work as the calculating mind. To accept the latter and reject the former is to say, in effect, that God did well in one case but fumbled badly in another.

The Bible is much too rich and variegated in its presentation of God's message to man to be squeezed into any kind of narrow mold that happens to appeal to us in our particular century. The only intelligent and spiritually mature way to read the Bible is to let it speak in its own way while we listen carefully to the nuances of its message. And this holds true in a very special sense for the Book of Revelation.

Bible scholars recognize that the apocalyptic outlook which John manifested in his writing developed its own distinct literary form, unlike anything else in the history of world literature. They also agree that his composition of Revelation is one of the finest examples of this literary form. Even your first reading of the book alerts you to the fact that you are being confronted with something quite out of the ordinary.

The Artist's Touch

Revelation resembles poetry in the way it uses words to appeal to the imagination and the feelings, but it is not limited to poetic forms. From another point of view, Revelation resembles the work of an imaginative painter in its use of images to convey meanings, but the canvas that is used here is the mind of the reader. From yet another perspective, Revelation reminds

37

one of the symphonic composer and his use of themes and counterpoints and his progression toward a grand climax. And one may also find in this book the fascination with structure and numbers that is characteristic of the mathematician and the architect.

As this suggests, Revelation is much more like a work of art than an ordinary discourse. It is written in a simple Greek that often violates the rules of classical Greek grammar and syntax, but it possesses a kind of primitive power and clarity that leaves an unforgettable impression. The intricate structure of the book defies a close logical analysis but evokes only admiration for the author's artistic imagination. At times the imagery and symbolism of Revelation may threaten to overwhelm you, but the artist-author never seems to lose control of his techniques. And Revelation seems to be able to touch every kind of human emotion from utter fear and stark despair to ecstatic joy and untroubled peace.

Impact

Two requirements are essential in our understanding and appreciation of art; both of these are equally important in the study of Revelation. First we need "impact." This means that we must submit willingly and often to the impact which the work of art makes upon all our responsive faculties. In the case of Revelation, we need to read the book frequently, until its various parts and the book as a whole become familiar and can be easily recalled.

When you read for impact, you do not need to be overly concerned with what each specific passage means. It is better to let your imagination run along freely, open to the abundance of impressions that the book can make upon your receptive mind. Nor should you feel obliged to read a certain amount each time. Half an hour spent in meditating on a single verse may sometimes be a far better investment than the rigid "one chapter a day" scheme. Also, there is no reason why Revelation should always be read in strict sequence from beginning to end. This book lends itself to browsing. As a work of art it does not

REVELATION 7:1–3

present a strictly logical argument that must be followed step by step. Of course, reading the book from beginning to end is valuable, especially after the parts have become somewhat familiar. This is like stepping back to examine a painting after looking at the details, to get a better view of the whole.

As you read Revelation a second time, try using a different translation. If you know another language, read a translation in that tongue. Your purpose in varying the text that you use is not to compare different translations to get the most exact rendering of the original but rather to get the benefit of many attempts to express in modern language what John wrote.

Structure

The second essential element in learning to understand and appreciate a work of art is indicated by the word "structure." A good work of art is always carefully planned so that all its parts form a structured whole. It is really impossible to go very far in understanding the artist's meaning until this structure is discovered. For instance, a Bach fugue may seem like nothing more than a monotonous and even annoying sequence of sounds until we learn to understand its contrapuntal structure and thus can recognize the subtle progression of its movements. We may have some fine impressions from a Rembrandt painting without knowing much about its structure, but our enjoyment of it will be enhanced tremendously when we learn to see how the parts are related to the picture as a whole.

There are, of course, many kinds of structures in art. Some of these may be very simple and undemanding. Others are highly complex and challenging—but also very rewarding when their subtle and marvelous patterns begin to become clear. It will not take you very long to discover that Revelation has a very complex structure—so complex, in fact, that you may feel there is no structure at all.

Revelation is different from other biblical writings. It has neither a closely reasoned argument nor an orderly procedure from the beginning, through the middle, to the end. Any attempt to make a detailed, consistent outline of the book, such as can be done very successfully with some other biblical books, is bound to be highly personal. There is some advantage to be gained from trying your hand at outlining the book and comparing your notes with others. Don't, however, insist on freezing these ideas of structure into a permanent form. John's structure is more psychological than it is logical, more dramatic than it is pedantic.

Keeping Notes

As you study, you may find it helpful to keep a written record or diary of your reactions and insights. There is a simple psychological wisdom behind this suggestion. Ideas and impressions are not really our own until we are able to express them in our own words. Writing them down is the best way to do this. Your notebook or diary can be very informal. In fact, it will be useful if it is kept that way. Write down questions that you want to have answered, unfamiliar words that can be looked up in the dictionary and their meanings noted, meanings that occur to you as John's word-pictures pass before your mind's eye. It may be interesting to attempt to sketch the way you picture some of the various scenes. The Hungarian-American artist, Lajos Szalay, whose art appears in this book, did just that. Compare your reactions with his. Your notes, sketches, and reactions are all part of your involvement with Revelation. The more involved you become with its important message, the more you will feel the impact of the book in your life.

"All those whom I love I correct and discipline. Therefore, shake off your complacency and repent. See, I stand knocking at the door. If anyone listens to my voice and opens the door, I will go into his house and dine with him, and he with me. As for the victorious, I will give him the honor of sitting beside me on my throne, just as I myself won the victory and have taken my seat beside my Father on his throne."

REVELATION 3:19–21
J. B. Phillips translation

5 · *The Structure of Revelation*

N READING Revelation, as in reading any other part of the Bible, do not be overly concerned with the division of the text into chapters and verses. These arbitrary divisions are very useful, of course, when we want to refer to particular passages. But as you may know, these numbering devices were added many centuries after the books of the Bible were written to make it easier for copyists to produce additional manuscripts. The arbitrary divisions unfortunately do not always reflect the natural units of thought within the writings. Several modern translations of the Bible put the verse and chapter numbers in the margin, so that the text can be read like any other book—paragraph by paragraph.

Preface and Epilogue

An author usually writes his ideas in natural units of thought, in a series of sentences or paragraphs that have a common theme or purpose and form a unit of the larger whole. Thus, as we begin reading Revelation, we find that the first three verses of the first chapter form a kind of preface to the whole book. Here it is made clear that the message of the book comes from God and that it is important to pay attention to it.

44

Skipping next to the end of the book, we can see that the last sixteen verses (22:6–21) form an epilogue. Here the words of the preface about the origin and the importance of the book's message are repeated in expanded form, with some final words of exhortation and encouragement to the Christians who read it. Between these extremes, then, lies the main body of the work.

Three Divisions

As we examine the main body of Revelation, we will discover that it divides naturally into three main parts of unequal length. The first and shortest of these parts has as its main theme John's initial vision of the risen and exalted Christ (1:4–20). After some introductory statements John relates here how the message came to him on the island of Patmos "on the Lord's day," and then goes on to describe the exalted Christ whom he saw in his vision.

The next main part (2:1—3:22) is in the form of special messages to each of seven churches in the province of Asia. Each church is identified by the name of the town in which it was located, and all the towns that are mentioned are known to have existed at the time of the writing of Revelation. There is no doubt that John believes in the necessity of the church to unite Christians in their common witness to Christ. Even though congregations may have serious faults, they are important in God's plan for his people. The messages reveal detailed knowledge of each of the seven congregations, and the picture of different levels of achievement and spiritual health which is drawn here makes it quite obvious that John had real congregations in mind.

The last and by far the longest main part (4:1—22:5) contains what at first sight may appear as a bewildering succession of images that seem to have little direct bearing on any actual life situation. The visions are about "what must take place after this" (4:1), and the perspective of these visions is neither Patmos nor the province of Asia but the transcendent realm of heaven. It is this third main part, which comprises

45

the major portion of the Book of Revelation, that is the most difficult and challenging.

The Key

One of the first things to catch our attention as we begin reading Revelation is the repetition of the number seven in each of the three main parts. In John's initial vision of the exalted Christ there are "seven spirits" (1:4), "seven churches" (1:11), "seven golden lampstands" (1:12), and "seven stars" (1:16). The messages to the churches are seven in number, and it seems possible to discern seven parts in each of the messages. And this is not all: in the last main part there seem to be seven main visions of the future, and each of these main visions seems to have seven parts.

John's constant reuse of the number seven cannot be accidental. The number may well be a key to the structure of the whole book and hence also a key to the interpretation of the message of Revelation. But why the number seven, and how are we to understand the meaning of this use of seven?

Symbolic Numbers

To modern people, numbers are useful but otherwise quite prosaic devices used for calculation and other such purposes. They have little or no meaning apart from the things they represent. But this was not so in antiquity. The Egyptians, Babylonians, and Greeks who first learned to use numbers in advanced calculations were tremendously impressed by the seemingly magic power of numbers. For instance, the ancient Greek philosopher Pythagoras is reported to have said that "all things are numbers," and he assigned special numbers to such things as male and female, marriage and justice. Another Greek philosopher, Plato, later developed a theory of the universe, its origin and structure, based on numerical relations and abstract geometrical figures.

This fascination with numbers was further stimulated by the fact that in much of the ancient world there were no special symbols to represent numbers; the letters of the regular

46

alphabet were used for this purpose. The results of this were that every name could have a numerical value, and the number of a name could also be used as a kind of code. An example of this can be found in Revelation in the passage where it is said that the number of the beast is "six hundred and sixty-six" (13:18). As will be seen later, this turns out to be a code name for the Roman emperor Nero.

The Completeness of Seven

Certain numbers, especially among the first ten, were universally believed to contain or convey special power and meaning. This is particularly true of the number seven, which was associated with completeness and perfection throughout the ancient world. Perhaps for this reason most ancient civilizations considered seven to be a lucky number. Seven was used prominently in many of the basic understandings about the world in which they lived. For instance, the ancient astronomers had identified seven moving planets in the sky (including the sun and the moon), and this suggested to them a kind of astrological perfection. The musical scale, which figured prominently in Pythagorean and Platonic speculation about the nature of the universe, had seven notes. In the Bible we are told that the creation of the world took place in seven days or periods of time, the last of which was the day of rest after everything had been completd. The Hebrews also counted the passing of time in seven time units—the days of the week. In the Law of Moses there were provisions for setting aside each seventh year as a time in which the soil of the land should be given a rest, old· debts settled, land restored to its rightful owners, and the renewal of life celebrated in various ways. Many important tasks reported in the Old Testament, such as the erection of the tabernacle in the wilderness and the building of Solomon's temple, were completed in seven time units. And very sacred events, such as a solemn oath (Genesis 21:28–32) or a religious ritual (Leviticus 4:6), also involved the number seven. Jesus stressed this symbolism when he sent out seventy disciples to preach the gospel.

REVELATION 8:12

Both John and those who first read Revelation were very well acquainted with this use and meaning of the number seven. In employing this number in such a prominent way, John obviously meant to say something that his readers could grasp quite easily. And the first and most direct effect of using the number seven in this way was to alert the readers to the fact that Revelation does not simply deal with a local and temporary problem, such as the persecution of the Christian church in the province of Asia. John is saying, rather, that he wants to show how this problem is related to the whole future of the kingdom of God on earth. He is taking the complete view, one which extends from Alpha to Omega (the first and last letters of the Greek alphabet), from the beginning to the end (Revelation 22:13).

The Subtleness of Seven

It is not too difficult for us to understand this part of John's use of the number seven symbolically. But we should not think that numbers only represent discrete entities, or we may miss a very important part of John's meaning. For instance, we may quickly conclude that the seven great visions of the future, described by John in the third main part of his book, must represent seven successive time periods, after which the world will come to a dramatic end. There have been some interpreters of Revelation who even thought that they could relate these seven visions to specific periods and events in Western history and on this basis calculate the calendar date of the end of the present world.

John's use of the number seven in Revelation points to a much more subtle meaning. As we have noted there are not only seven visions of the future, but each of these seven visions contains seven parts, and the seventh part of the preceding vision is the beginning of the next vision. For instance, the breaking of the seventh seal (8:1) is the introduction of the vision of the seven trumpets (8:1 ff.). Likewise, the blowing of the seventh trumpet (11:15–19) leads directly into the vision of the seven portents (12:1 ff.). And the seventh

49

portent (15:1) is the beginning of the seven bowls of wrath (16:1 ff.).

The effect of this is something like a set of Chinese boxes, one nested within the other. Or, to use a more contemporary illustration, John's seven visions of the future are like a stroboscopic photograph in which successive phases of a movement are superimposed on each other, so that the movement is seen at one glance from beginning to end. The beginning and end are not thousands of years apart but are one and the same.

The Use of Four

The number four also figures prominently in Revelation (see, for example, 4:6b–8; 6:1–8). This number has a special relationship to the number seven, something which John appears to have been aware of. If we have a row of seven pebbles and count four from either end, we will in each case arrive at the pebble in the center. Likewise, if we think of an arch made of seven cut stones, the fourth one would be the keystone that keeps the arch from collapsing. Both of these illustrations suggest something other than a straight succession of events or a linear progression from beginning to end. They suggest a significant relationship.

The number four also occupied an important role in ancient thought. People spoke of the four corners of the earth and the four major winds that blew across the earth. They thought that there were four basic elements—fire, air, water, and earth— out of which all other things were made. And there were the four seasons of the year, the four phases of the moon, and the four harmonic notes of the scale. John's use of the number four also brings to mind the prophet Ezekiel, the Old Testament apocalyptic writer, whom John must have studied carefully and from whom he has borrowed some of his symbols. Ezekiel speaks in his visions of something that looked like wheels within wheels and that went in four directions (Ezekiel 10:9–14). This phrase, wheels within wheels, could also be applied to the visions of John as a description of how they are related to each other.

Different Views of History

Sometimes historians and others speak of the "horizontal" and the "vertical" views of history. In the horizontal view attention is directed to the flow of events through the years and centuries; what comes before and what follows after is of great importance. In the vertical view, on the other hand, attention is given to what may be considered a cross section of a culture at a given time. Using this kind of distinction in speaking about John's visions of the future, we could say that John's use of numerical symbolism in these visions suggests that in some subtle way the horizontal and the vertical views coincide or come together.

This would mean that John's visions of the future are descriptions of contemporary life, regardless of the time to which one refers. The apocalyptic view of a conflict between the "present age" and the "new age," between Babylon and New Jerusalem, between Antichrist and Christ, must be understood as describing the situation in any age. The dramatic confrontation of good and evil that John speaks about not only happened at the time he lived—it also happens at all times, in the hearts of men as well as in the culture to which they belong. From this point of view, history is not just a passage through time from beginning to end but an eternal *now* in a historic setting. Theological ideas such as creation, the fall of man through sin, judgment, redemption, and restoration are elements of daily human experience.

A person confronted for the first time with this view of history and this interpretation of Revelation may hesitate for several reasons. In the first place, he may not recognize in his own life and in the culture to which he belongs anything so dramatic and titanic as the struggle between good and evil described by John in Revelation. Second, he may point out that John himself seems to be concerned with particular historical situations. For instance, the Babylon whose fall John describes in such moving language in the eighteenth chapter is clearly a code name for ancient Rome. And it has already been mentioned that the beast's number is a code for the name of Nero. Finally, one may ask if this view does not run counter to the ancient belief that there will be a final judgment at the end of history, at which Christ will come again "to judge the quick and the dead."

Here it is important to consider again the suggestion that Revelation must be understood as a work of art. A true artist is not just one who does clever things with his materials. His main concern is to point to what is really significant in the mass of details that influence our lives. He often does this on a heroic scale, both to make his meaning clear and to evoke in his audience a sense of the significance and the urgency that he himself has experienced. If he is successful in this, we come away from an exposure to his work feeling that we have seen our own existence in a new and clearer light—even if there is no direct connection between the subject matter of his work of art and the details of our own experience. We do not dismiss Shakespeare's *Hamlet* because we ourselves are not of royal Danish blood and do not live in a medieval castle. *Hamlet* is great because it has a message for all people. In the same way the dramatic scenes of Revelation, so remote from life in our modern culture, may have a meaningful message for us.

The Last Judgment

The question concerning what is usually taken to be the traditional belief in a last judgment is not an easy one to answer. One can say with assurance that the main concern in this belief has been to remind human beings that they are responsible for their conduct of life. The simple view of a final gathering of all living and dead in a given place on earth is rather difficult to fit in with the rest of our understanding of life. In itself the vision of a judgment seat, the opening of the books, and the final judgment is a vivid expression of the call to responsible conduct, but the literal interpretation of this as something that will take place in the historic future gives rise to all kinds of difficulties. It is far better to follow a suggestion in the Gospel of John and think of judgment as something that is always taking place (John 3:18).

A Word of Warning

This discussion of the structure of Revelation is meant to provide only some general suggestions to help you in your exploration of the book. And a word of warning is in order here. Having discovered the numerical symbolism of Revelation and the "hidden" meaning of some other symbols, you may be tempted to think that the whole book is as tightly organized as a crossword puzzle and that each part and each symbol have a well-defined place and meaning. This is not so, and any attempt to force these elements into a neat pattern may lead to a distortion of the book and its message.

Remember that John worked as an artist and that all true art leaves much room for what the spectator himself contributes to the experience. For instance, one of the most dramatic statements in Revelation is that about the "silence in heaven for about half an hour" (8:1). But who can give a precise meaning to this statement? If our imagination is captured by this silence, we may sense something of eternal significance; but there will also be something intensely personal in our response, and the distance between John on the island of Patmos and us in the middle of the twentieth century will begin to fade away.

6 · The Center of Revelation

GOOD work of art has not only structure but also a center or focal point which holds the various parts together and gives them a meaning that they could not otherwise have. In a piece of music this focal point may be a melodic theme that appears and reappears in different ways to gather together the embellishments and variations that the composer has used to give a fullness to his work. In a painting it may be a figure or a suggested action to which the eye is invariably drawn and to which the other parts of the picture seem to point. One of the most meaningful aspects of studying a work of art is discovering this focal point and seeing how it sheds light and bestows meaning on each of the parts that make up the whole. To miss the center is to miss the primary reason for the art's existence.

Christ the Center

If Revelation is approached in this manner as a work of art, it is of vital importance to discover its focal point or center. And this is not difficult to find. John presents his theme, his focal point, in the initial vision of "one like a son of man" (1:13) who "in his right hand . . . held seven stars" (1:16).

THE CENTER OF REVELATION

Our imagination is taxed beyond capacity as we try to envision the exalted Christ that John describes in this section (1:12–20). John's frequent use of the word "like" serves to warn us here that he does not mean to be understood literally when he speaks of feet "like burnished bronze" and eyes "like a flame of fire." He is using earthly language to describe what is beyond description. The result becomes grotesque if we try to take him literally and forget that he is using similes and metaphors. But if we read this passage the way John intended, we are confronted with an almost unbearably brilliant picture of the risen and exalted Christ.

One thing is clear immediately here. The Christ to whom John introduces his readers is more than the historical Jesus of Nazareth, the friend of little children, the healer and master teacher, the moral ideal of man, and the humble servant of all. The royal bearing of John's Christ is unmistakable; he is seen as "the first and the last, and the living one" (1:17–18). He is the one in whom the past, the present, and the future come together. And as such he is both the lord of the church and the lord of all history.

Lord of the Church

The role of Christ as the lord of the church is the special theme of the next main section of John's book (2:1—3:22). Christ knows well the character and life of each congregation and the position and problems of each individual member. He is fully aware of the frailty and fragmentariness of human existence; he is exceedingly sympathetic to those who struggle under these conditions. But it is also abundantly clear that Christ does not tolerate any form of counterfeit Christianity. Those who have the name of being alive but are dead (3:1), or who are lukewarm (3:16), have no place in the church of Christ. Christ is willing to meet every repentant backslider with the full measure of his restoring grace, but he will not abide those who remain uncommitted. As John describes the situation, it is impossible to be or remain a Christian by following the path of least resistance.

Lord of History

The role of Christ as the lord of the world and the lord of history is the special theme of the third main part of Revelation. It is important to note here the shift of perspective as John begins his description of the seven visions of the future. John is invited to enter an open door into heaven and from that vantage point observe details of "what must take place after this" (4:1).

John is here serving notice to his readers that what he is about to discuss is not accessible to ordinary human experience and common-sense judgments. This has two important and significant implications.

In the first place, John is saying that if we want to understand what is really happening in the world then we must be prepared to go beyond what appears to us as the face value of facts and look for some meaning that is not obvious.

In the second place, this means that we must be ready to accept the idea that there is a reality other than that which we encounter daily in sensory experience—a world beyond the world of time and space. This is not to say that we must accept some naïve view of a heaven in some "place" other than this earth, but it does mean that we acknowledge that there is a realm of the spirit which transcends ordinary experiences and meaning. If we are not willing to accept these two propositions implied by John's statement that he was asked to "come up hither" (4:1), we shall not have much success in penetrating the meaning of his seven visions of the future. We must take the spiritual dimension into account.

The Lamb

To understand the role of Christ as the lord of the world and the lord of history, it is also important to notice the image of Christ as he is introduced by John in this role. The one who came forward to break the seals of the scrolls that contained within them the pattern of things to come was seen as "a Lamb standing, as though it had been slain" (5:6). The importance of this image is emphasized by the fact that the

Lamb was the only one in heaven and on earth found worthy to open these seals, and he was found worthy because he was slain (5:9). The reference to Christ as the Lamb occurs more than two-dozen times in the seven visions of the future and is clearly the dominant image of Christ in this part of the book. The meaning of this symbol is not difficult to understand. Christ as the Lamb is the redeemer of the world, as is expressed so beautifully in the ecstatic hymn sung by the attendants around the throne of God in heaven (5:9–10). This view of Christ is the "new song" that is both the key to the future and the theme of the new age. The sacrificial lamb is a familiar image both in the Old and the New Testaments. But we notice that the vision of Christ as the Lamb in John's book is by no means that image of the submissive and silent lamb led to the slaughter which Isaiah the Hebrew prophet described (Isaiah 53:7). The Lamb of Revelation possesses "power and wealth and wisdom and might and honor and glory and blessing" (Revelation 5:12), seven great attributes that are never lost sight of in all the turbulence of the unfolding visions. Whether the Lamb is breaking the seals of the scroll (5:1—8:5), leading the first fruits of the redeemed (14:1–5), subduing the forces of evil when they attack him (17:13–14), or receiving the New Jerusalem as his bride (21:9–14), his regal bearing is always apparent. Christ, the lord of the world and the lord of history, is not lost in the image of Christ as the redeemer of the world.

Other Images of Christ

The royal role of Christ is underscored in other images, such as that of the rider on the white horse who leads the armies in heaven in a conquest of the nations of the world (19:11–21). The sight of a king or a general riding at the head of an army going into battle was doubtless one of the most familiar and vivid symbols of power and authority in the ancient world.

For John's original readers, who may have been tempted to think that the hostile Roman Empire represented the ultimate

REVELATION 12:1–17

in power, the image of Christ as one who "will rule [the nations] with a rod of iron" (19:15) was a heartening reminder that their oppressors were not to have the last word in the days ahead.

God the Father

The picture of Christ painted in Revelation is not complete until some thought has been given to his relationship with God. God—who is called "the Lord God" (1:8), "the Lord God Almighty" (4:8), and "our Lord" (11:15)—is mentioned quite often in Revelation. But except for the beautiful passage toward the end of the book which says that God will wipe away every tear from the eyes of those who have suffered faithfully to the end (21:3–4), Revelation does not ascribe a very active role to God. The dominant image of God is that of "one seated on the throne" (4:2), somewhat august and remote. He is the creator and sustainer of all things and thus also the one whom all creation worships (4:11), and he will be the center in the New Jerusalem (21:22–23). In his place upon the throne in heaven, God is surrounded by twenty-four adoring elders and four living creatures (4:4–7), and he is served by angels who carry out special missions (8:2).

Undoubtedly the picture in the back of John's mind as he describes God in this way is that of an Oriental potentate sitting on his throne in the royal splendor of his court, surrounded by admiring attendants and ruling his realm through his ministers. Christ is said to be "his Christ" (11:15), and God is referred to as Christ's "Father" (14:1). Obviously, Christ's place in this picture is that of the crown prince who is his father's right-hand aide and special deputy throughout the realm.

This picture of God was a thoroughly meaningful one to John's original readers, who had been nurtured on tales of such splendor and instinctively knew the symbolic power of such a picture. As an artistic symbol it can also be meaningful to modern people, so long as they do not interpret it too literally.

Handling a Problem

Those who are inclined to interpret this image literally will find that they are confronted in Revelation with what seems like two divine beings, God almighty and Christ his Son, both of whom demand man's utmost loyalty and unreserved worship. This is distressing in their understanding of the one God whom they feel called to worship and serve. Some people have tried to find the solution to this difficulty by developing a kind of radical Unitarianism which rejects the concept of the Trinity, the idea of God's incarnation in Christ, the doctrine of redemption, and—virtually the whole message of Revelation. Others, who would be horrified at the thought of accepting the Unitarian position and ignoring the lordship of Christ, handle the problem by drifting into something that some modern thinkers have called "Christocentric Unitarianism." In this view, God whom we know as Father and God whom we know as the Holy Spirit, the two other members of the Trinity, fade into the background and Christ alone becomes the center of faith and worship. If at the same time the Christ of worship is virtually synonymous with Jesus of Nazareth, confusion and errors are compounded.

Neither of these forms of Unitarianism are necessary to reconcile John's picture of the relationship of Christ to God with our basic Christian faith. If we keep in mind that the picture itself is a symbol borrowed from a given cultural and political environment, it is not difficult to see that loyalty to the crown prince is also loyalty to his royal father. In this sense they are not two persons vying for human adoration and support but two representatives or manifestations of the same authority. We find this idea expressed very clearly in the Gospel of John: "I and the Father are one" (John 10:30); and "He who believes in me, believes not in me but in him who sent me" (John 12:44).

If we look beyond the images of Christ in the Book of Revelation and try to formulate their meaning in nonsymbolic language, we can say that John's purpose is to show that God is redemptively present in the world and that this redemptive presence is the key to the meaning of all history. The philosophy of history which John teaches is a philosophy of redemption—God is actively seeking to help his people by destroying evil on their behalf. All things that happen are in some way related to this central fact.

Interpreting Symbols

Some further implications of this understanding of the message of Revelation will be explored later. In the meantime it must be stressed that Christ as the center or focal point of Revelation provides the key to the interpretation of all the other symbols in the book. Some of these symbols are quite meaningless if they are regarded apart from their relationship to the central symbol of Christ as redeemer. In studying these symbols it is always good to ask: How does this relate to the focal point? For instance, John's vision of the mother of harlots (17:1–6), also identified as Babylon, is obviously a symbol of ancient Rome. But why this image and what does it mean? The harlot, is, of course, a symbol of infidelity and defilement. But John is not speaking merely of sexual vice. He is saying that in the world there is an alternative to loyalty to Christ, something else that attracts man and makes a bid for his allegiance. This is the city of man, built on human greed and lust, as opposed to the city of God, the New Jerusalem and the bride of the Lamb. A choice between these two confronts everyone. And John makes it clear that he who chooses the city of man as the meaning of his existence will someday discover that he has made a radically wrong choice (18:9–10). As they contemplate the ruins of the city of man, the feelings of those who have chosen this city can be compared with the restrained but jubilant mood attending the appearance of the New Jerusalem looking like a bride adorned for her husband (21:1–4).

Thus you will find that each symbol used by John acquires proper meaning and more depth as it is seen in relationship to the central theme of Revelation, the Christ who is the lord of the world and the lord of history and whose role as such

THE BOOK OF REVELATION

is the Lamb—the Redeemer. Using this key to the interpretation of John's book will not make the reading of his visions of the future simple and easy, but it will give you the right perspective and indicate the kind of questions you should be asking about the meaning of these symbols in terms of your own life situations and your membership in the people of God.

7 · The Church in the World

CHRISTIANS of all ages have acknowledged Jesus Christ as their Lord and as the lord of the church, but they have done so with the uneasy feeling that they were living in a hostile world where the lordship of Christ was not recognized and the flow of events seemed utterly incompatible with the meaning of Christ and his church. Where this feeling is dominant, it is easy to become rather pessimistic about the possibilities of life in this world, to think of this existence as a "vale of tears" in which we wait, sometimes impatiently, for the real life to begin in the hereafter. There have been times in the past when Christians thought that the best thing they could do was to withdraw and set up isolated Christian communities far removed from the secular cities of the world.

On the other hand, there have been times—and perhaps our own time is one—when little or no distinction was made between the life of the Christian and the life of the man of the world. In such times the confession that Christ is the lord of the church tends to become merely a formal statement with little real power and meaning. At such times the church may attempt to exert influence and gain power over the social and cultural life, but it does so as one power block among other power blocks, and may also resort to methods that are no different from the methods used by secular groups.

Revelation challenges both of these alternatives!

The People of God

John's message is that the church can remain the church only if it remains true to its calling as the church of Christ, the people of God. On the other hand, his confident assertion that the lord of the church is also the lord of the world and the lord of history makes it impossible for the Christian to look with complete pessimism or total indifference at what is happening in the world. The Christian is encouraged to watch "the signs of the times" (Matthew 16:2–4) and also to participate with Christ in the task of bringing about the coming of the new age amid the disintegration of the old age. He cannot look upon the church as serving merely his own needs, for it serves the needs of all God's people. And he cannot withdraw from participation in the world if he realizes that his Lord is active in the world where his people live. He has a responsibility to be Christ's active witness through his participation in the church fellowship right where he is in God's world.

The role of Christ as the lord of the church and the lord of the world and of history, so strongly emphasized in Revelation, gives new depth and meaning to the relationship between the world and the church, and to the Christian's relationship to both of these.

The role of Christ as the lord of the church is the main theme of the messages to the seven churches (2:1—3:22). John leaves no doubt in his readers' minds about Christ's position in this regard. The exalted Christ who "walks among the seven golden lampstands" (2:1) is the very image of the sovereign Lord. This vision should banish any thought that the church is merely a human organization run by human beings for human purposes. It is *his* church, not ours; we do not invite him as our guest but come as his guests to participate in the life of the church.

Measuring a Congregation

The consequences of this understanding of the church become apparent as we read the messages to the seven churches. It means, first of all, that the church as a whole and each local congregation must subject themselves to critical scrutiny at all times. Self-criticism is a vital part of the life of the church, and any church that begins to think that it has reached a state where self-criticism is no longer needed is in a precarious position. Furthermore, the criteria to be used in this self-criticism are not those that we normally apply to group life and institutions. For instance, the church in Ephesus (2:1–7) had been doing well in many respects: the members had been working hard and with much patience, they had shown great discernment in testing and rejecting counterfeit teachers, and they had shown courage in opposing false doctrine. Yet they were in grave need of repentance and in danger of losing their status as a church of Christ. The fault of the church was not one that a casual visitor might detect: the abandonment of "the love you had at first" (2:4). But beneath the surface of apparent success lay serious problems.

As we look at the other messages to the churches, we find that there are only two, Smyrna (2:8–11) and Philadelphia (3:7–13), that escape serious criticism, and these are also the two that can show very little outward evidence of success, for they are poor (2:9) and have little strength (3:8). Some of the sharpest words are spoken to the church in Laodicea (3:14–22), smugly satisfied with itself, and to the church in Sardis (3:1–6), resting on its reputation.

The Whole Church

An impartial reader of these messages may well conclude that if these seven churches represent the life of the Christian church on earth there is only a slim chance that the church will survive, to say nothing of achieving a triumphant victory over the forces of evil. And this raises also the question of how we are to understand the larger meaning of these messages to the seven churches.

As has already been indicated, there were a number of other churches in the province of Asia in addition to those John named specifically. For instance, there were Christian congregations in Colossae and Hierapolis (see Colossians 4:13), each just a few miles from Laodicea. Other cities, such as Tralles and Magnesia, are also known to have been the homes of Christian believers. Obviously John must have had a special purpose in mind when he selected those seven particular churches to describe.

If we draw a line on the map through the seven cities in the order in which they are named, we find that we have followed a roughly circular route through what were doubtless the most important parts of the province of Asia. If John's book was sent along this route, it would reach the greatest number of people in the shortest period of time, and this fact may have played a part in the selection and naming of the churches. But the fact that exactly seven churches were named, seen against the many other uses of the number seven in Revelation, suggests that John had some other idea in mind than just the practical problem of spreading the word of his visions as quickly as possible. The symbolic meaning of seven as "wholeness" suggests that he is speaking of the church at all times and in all places.

What Can Happen

There are those who have thought that the seven churches in Revelation represent seven distinct periods in the history of the church, and much ingenious thought has gone into the attempt to explain this theory. But this kind of interpretation only invites the same problems that we encounter if we try to understand John's seven visions of the future as distinct historical events or periods. It is much more in harmony with John's style and purpose as an apocalyptic writer to look upon his description of the seven churches as a candid picture of what can happen in church life at all times and in all places.

Can we say that any church in any time is free of the danger that threatened the church in Ephesus, where the

66

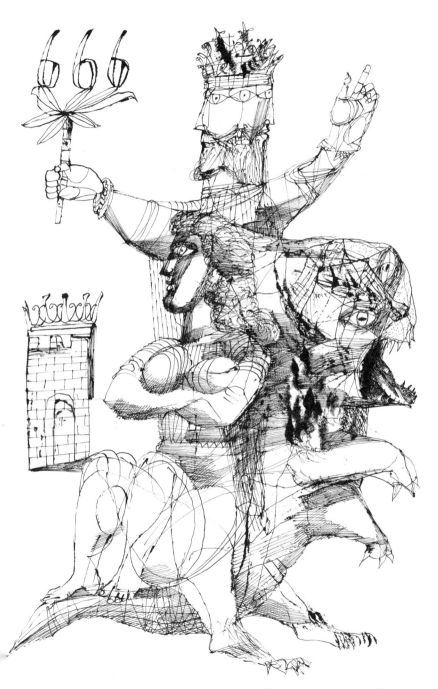

REVELATION 13:11–18

initial loving relation to God and man became lost in the institutional program? Is there not always a danger that a church, enjoying success in the community, can become smug and satisfied with itself in much the same way that this happened to the church in Laodicea?

Typical Conditions

Is the picture that John draws of the seven churches to be understood as typical of church life in the world then? Two things must be kept in mind as we attempt to answer this question. In the first place, Christ's church is not some sort of ethereal body set apart from ordinary human life. The church exists in concrete human communities such as Ephesus and Laodicea, and is subject to the conditions and circumstances that affect life in these communities. It does not stand outside the historical process, but is a part of this process; it is not isolated from the cultural, social, and political situation in which it finds itself, but is deeply involved. Many of the faults for which John's seven churches are criticized can be traced to local conditions that existed in the communities where the church members lived.

But, on the other hand, the life of the church is not derived from the community of which it is a part. The church does not just reflect or express the concerns of a given community; and it is not there just to bring into focus the values that a given community holds dear. The church is to reflect and express the meaning of Christ in human life; and, as John makes abundantly clear in Revelation, the meaning of Christ in human life is the meaning of redemption.

Criticism and Repentance

The idea of redemption implies a judgment upon the world of which the church is a part. It is impossible for the follower of Christ to accept the world as it is, and this applies just as much to the world within the church as the world outside the church. As the criticisms of the seven churches show clearly, Christians are constantly tempted to make room for worldly elements within the church. In one sense this cannot be avoided, since the church is in the world and takes part in the life of the community to which it belongs. The real danger arises when the church begins to hallow these worldly elements, the Balaams (2:14–15) and Jezebels (2:20), that seem both harmless and attractive to people whose spiritual sensitivities have become dulled. John recognizes that there are external dangers threatening the church, such as the "synagogue of Satan" (2:9) and many kinds of "tribulation" (2:10). But the major threat to the church is always internal: the erosion of spiritual life that may take place while the church members are hardly aware of what is happening.

The normal, permanent attitude of the living church is therefore one of self-examination, self-criticism, confession, repentance, and renewal. And the example of the Laodicean church suggests that this criticism and repentance may well concern itself with the things in which a church takes special pride. This gives new depth to the paradoxical statement in the message to the church in Smyrna, that there is richness in poverty (2:9).

Insofar as it illustrates the need for criticism and repentance in the church at all times, John's picture of the seven churches is indeed typical of all church life. But it would be wrong to assume that in these seven vignettes of congregational problems John has given a complete catalog of the possibilities of failure. The dangers for the churches in the province of Asia were related to conditions in that part of the world at that time. The dangers for the churches in North America are related to the conditions of life as they exist here and now. But the meaning of these dangers is always the same: that something else—and it does not matter what—diverts attention from Christ, who is the true life and meaning of the church wherever it is.

Redemptive Power

At the end of each of the seven messages John speaks about "him who conquers." But the reader of these messages may

69

wonder if anyone will conquer in the face of the external and internal dangers threatening the life of the church. John has a clear answer to this. The possibility of survival and conquest is not contingent on any human power or ability but on the redemptive power of Christ. The dazzling vision of the victorious, exalted Christ in the first chapter is connected to each of the seven churches. It is the Christ who was seen "in the midst of the [seven] lampstands" (1:13), who "held seven stars" (1:16), and who is addressing the church in Ephesus (2:1). It is he who described himself to John as "the first and the last" (1:17) who speaks to the church in Smyrna (2:8). In the same meaningful way John uses elements of the original vision of the exalted Christ in his introduction to all the churches.

The implication here is clear. The life of the church and the life of each Christian are grounded in Christ who has already conquered, and wherever hearts are turned to him victory is assured (see 3:4–5). There is no doubt about the outcome of the drama of salvation, for John stresses the conclusion in the beginning. This fact does not invite our complacency, however: for example, the emphasis at the end of each message to a church is on the person who will share in the ultimate victory, "he who has an ear" to hear; the Christian responds to the call of Christ through the Spirit to live loyally as a member of God's people.

Assurance of Victory

The assurance of ultimate victory through faith in the Christ who has already conquered can be a powerful boost to the Christian's morale in the face of the most difficult situations with which he is confronted. It enabled Christians, not so long after John wrote his book, to meet, calmly and even cheerfully, the threat of torture and death at the hands of Roman persecutors. But it may also tempt the Christian to think that he has no stake in what is happening in the world and to conclude that if he himself remains faithful to Christ his only other obligation is to wait patiently for the ultimate consummation of Christ's victory. One may even find con-firmation for such a passive approach in a hasty reading of Revelation and other biblical passages dealing with the future. But this is far from John's real meaning, as we can see when we examine more carefully the intricate structure of Revelation. He suggests that there is an intimate relationship between the seven churches and their life and the drama of world events pictured in the seven visions of the future. John does this by repeating the pattern of seven in the visions of the future, and also by repeating many of the symbols intro-duced in the initial vision of Christ and in the messages to the seven churches. Among these symbols are the tree of life (2:7; 22:2), the book of life (3:5; 13:8), the rod of iron (2:27; 12:5; 19:15), the white garments (3:5; 4:4; 6:11), and the New Jerusalem (3:12; 21:2). This is John's way of saying that the seven messages to the churches and the seven visions of the future belong together and must be seen from one perspective.

The implication here, too, is clear. To be a Christian in this world is to be involved in what is happening in this world. The church is not like a bomb shelter in which believers wait until the fury of the attack is spent. Christianity is not an invitation to withdraw from life but a call to participation in all the concerns of men. John's subtle linking of the vision of the exalted Christ, the messages to the seven churches, and the seven visions of the future can mean only one thing: the drama of redemption is encountered in all realms of life and experience. It can be seen on a huge scale in the historical process, on a somewhat smaller scale in the life of the church, and on a still smaller scale in the life of each human being.

8 · The Visions of the Future

THE messages to the seven churches
(2:1—3:22) form a rather simple pattern that you can
recognize with no difficulty. But this may not be the case
with the longest section of Revelation, the seven visions of
the future (4:1—22:5). The contrast between these two
parts is like the contrast between a simple New England
meetinghouse and an elaborate Gothic church with its inter-
lacing arches, buttresses, and vaulting. The reader of Revelation does not proceed far beyond the end of the third chapter before he develops an uncomfortable sensation that he has
lost his bearings and is about to be submerged by a welter of
impressions and ideas.

If the reader has had any previous experience in systematic
Bible study, he will naturally think that there must be some
kind of outline of this section that will help to bring order to
this seeming chaos. He may attempt to develop such an outline for himself. He may turn to various commentaries or
Bible handbooks for help. Here he will probably find that
hardly two writers agree on how to outline this part of John's
book. At this point he may be inclined to conclude that John
just didn't know what he was doing and that it is a difficult

task to try to make much sense out of John's visions of the future. This frustration may jeopardize his willingness to make Revelation a part of the biblical resources that he can turn to for inspiration and guidance.

On Your Own

But let us assume that the reader is willing to explore possibilities that he may not have considered before. He may be on the verge of making discoveries that will both enrich his spiritual life and enlarge his concept of the way God reveals himself to human beings.

The first step in this direction is to recognize that Revelation, especially the seven visions of the future, cannot be subjected to a precise logical analysis because it was not written that way and was not meant to be understood that way. As we have noted earlier, it is a kind of picture in which words take the place of pigments and brushes.

The next step is to make a deliberate attempt to deal directly with the impressions that the book makes without trying to organize and analyze its content. And here are several ways in which this can be done. As you read, your imagination will offer many other possibilities.

Sound Effects

The first suggestion is to read Revelation for "sound effects." Having our attention called to this possibility, we will soon discover that John was very much intrigued by sounds. There are, for instance, the sounds of voices all through the book. The voice that called him initially was "like a trumpet" (1:10), and so was the voice that invited him to come up into heaven to watch the unfolding of the seven visions of the future (4:1). From the throne in heaven there issued "voices and peals of thunder" (4:5). Again and again he refers to singing "with a loud voice" (5:12), "like the sound of many waters and like the sound of loud thunder" (14:2). The successive events of the seven visions of the future are introduced by stentorian voices described as "with a voice of

73

thunder" (6:1), "a loud voice" (14:9), "a mighty voice" (18:2), and "a great voice" (21:3). And there are the impatient voices of those who have suffered and who cry, "How long?" (6:10), as well as the frantic shouts of those who are calling to the mountains to fall upon them and hide them (6:16–17).

There are also other sound effects. The sound of trumpets reverberates throughout the book. And there is the intensely dramatic "silence in heaven for about half an hour" followed immediately by "peals of thunder, loud noises, flashes of lightning, and an earthquake" (8:1–5). There are seven thunders that speak about things to come, the content of which John is not permitted to reveal (10:4). There is reference to "the sound of harpers playing on their harps" (14:2), and the sound of people who weep and wail over the fallen city, Babylon (18:9).

The sounds of Revelation can provide the reader with a fascinating and moving way to get acquainted with the book. Sounds are great vehicles for communicating feelings. John's purpose was to stir the feelings of his readers so that they can catch the momentous significance of what he is disclosing.

Visual Effects

Revelation can also be read for "visual effects." That John is as intrigued by sights as he is by sounds is apparent in the initial vision of the exalted Christ. The metaphors and similes that he uses to describe this Christ combine to evoke an almost unbearably brilliant image (1:12–16). No less dazzling is John's description of what he saw when he entered the open door into heaven (4:2–11). Since this passage gives the perspective from which everything else in the seven visions of the future is to be seen, it will be good to read this often. The description of the New Jerusalem in the concluding vision (21:9–27) is also vivid. As we walk through a city gate "made of a single pearl" onto streets of "pure gold, transparent as glass," we can hardly avoid being touched by the ecstasy of John's experience.

THE VISIONS OF THE FUTURE

As we read Revelation, we soon become aware that most of the material in the seven visions of the future is visual in nature. Rather than speaking in theological or philosophical language, John draws verbal pictures. He does not simply say that Christ will overcome the opposition of his enemies and the enemies of the church, but he draws a picture of a rider on a white horse going into battle (19:11 ff.). Instead of defining the nature of evil, he describes a "beast rising out of the sea" (13:1 ff.) and a woman "arrayed in purple and scarlet" (17:4 ff.). Instead of speaking in abstract terms of the destruction of the city of man, he describes "the smoke of her burning" (18:9), and adds depth to this picture by giving a detailed inventory of the merchandise that has become useless with the destruction of the city (18:11–13). John's pictorial skill adds emphasis to his message.

Take Your Time

There is an abundance of these pictures in Revelation— brilliant, foreboding, sublime, grotesque, depressing, and inspiring. The hurried reader of John's book is in much the same position as the tourist who wants to make a quick trip through a famous art museum. After a while the mind tires and the eyes refuse to see. The situation is further complicated by the fact that it is sometimes hard to say where one picture ends and another begins.

The best advice we can follow here is that which is followed by the intelligent museum visitor: do a little at a time, and take your time. Pause long enough with each visual image to let the details of the picture emerge fully. For instance, in our first reading of John's description of heaven (4:2–11) we may overlook the "sea of glass, like crystal" that is before the throne of God. But the sense of distance conveyed by this image adds so much to the majestic sublimity of God upon his throne! Likewise, the splendor of John's New Jerusalem with its jasper walls, pearly gates, and streets of gold may keep one from noticing at first the significant detail that the gates of this city are never closed.

Each image, both of the splendors of heaven and the new age and of the evils and tribulations of this age, needs quiet and attentive meditation. And those with an artistic bent and a knack for drawing can have a wonderful time trying to put down on paper some of the things that John saw.

Exploring Feelings

A third kind of approach to Revelation is to explore the many feelings that are evoked. Good artist and reporter that he is, John never lets his own personality intrude into the pictures he draws. But he never hides the fact that he was deeply stirred by what he saw and that he expects his readers to be affected in the same way.

The book begins with the merest hint of the sense of loneliness that the prisoner on the island of Patmos must have felt as he was there by himself "on the Lord's day" when normally he would meet in worship with his fellow Christians. But this feeling is quickly overcome when he is confronted with the exalted Christ, and John was so overcome by this experience that he "fell at his feet as though dead" (1:17). He also relates how later he "wept much that no one was found worthy to open the scroll or to look into it" (5:3). And when he heard the angel announce the marriage supper of the Lamb, he "fell down at his feet to worship him" (19: 10), only to be reminded that God alone should be worshiped.

The exploration of the emotional impact of Revelation does not mean, however, that we should attempt to imitate John's feelings. Rather, we should be willing to respond directly to the emotional stimuli in the symbols and images used by John. And John's seven visions of the future have the power to engage the whole range of our emotional responses—from pure ecstasy to stark horror.

It is not coincidence that Revelation is often the favorite book of the "emotional sects" while it has been largely ignored by members of more traditional, conservative groups. The book does appeal in a unique way to feelings, in a way that few other books of the Bible do. And the fact that some of

REVELATION 14:6–11

these sectarian groups have misinterpreted and thus misused Revelation does not eliminate the possibility that they have been fundamentally correct in their willingness to respond emotionally to the message of John's book. At any rate, the answer to their mistake is not a tacit agreement to ignore Revelation but a willingness to become involved.

Emotional Involvement

The tendency in our modern Western culture to praise rationality and deprecate feelings is in large measure an inheritance from our Greek cultural ancestors. Socrates, Plato, Aristotle, the great teachers and shapers of Western thought, all agreed that reason is man's highest good and that emotions are apt to lead man astray. But in the Hebrew and biblical view of man, there is none of this great veneration of reason at the expense of feelings. Feelings are as important as reason in the total life of man. The Book of Psalms, for instance, reflects an almost infinite range of religious moods and feelings, and so do many of the prophetic writings.

Feelings are no less the result of God's creative endowment of man than is reason. Therefore, they are a vital part of the faculties with which man responds to God. And there comes a point in the reader's exploration of Revelation when he is confronted with the need to become emotionally involved if he is to become a participant in the events that John describes. It is one thing to read that "war arose in heaven, Michael and his angels fighting against the dragon" (12:7) and to speculate on what this could mean. It is quite another thing to be caught, emotionally speaking, in the middle of that fight, to sense the fury of the battle and the crucial importance of the outcome as far as your own struggles between good and evil are concerned.

Some of our greatest hymns reflect the experiences of people who have become emotionally involved in Revelation. In "Holy, Holy, Holy," Reginald Heber's immortal line "Casting down their golden crowns around the glassy sea" could only have been written by one whose feelings had been stirred by the scene that John describes in the fourth chapter of Revelation. Many other well-known hymns reflect the experiences of people who have caught glimpses of John's visions and have responded to what they saw.

As you become emotionally involved in Revelation, you will begin to feel the impact of those passages that depict the ecstasy, glory, and triumph of the kingdom of God. But it is not all glory and triumph. You will not sense the full meaning of these passages or of Revelation as a whole unless you also become familiar with the dark and gruesome passages that provide a counterpoint to the scenes of joy and happiness.

For instance, the rejoicing of the "great multitude which no man could number, from every nation, from all tribes and peoples and tongues" (7:9) becomes vastly more meaningful when it is seen against the background of the quaking fear of the kings and the strong as they cry out to the mountains to fall on them and hide them (6:12–17). Likewise, the full · power of the jubilant song of the elect with the Lamb of Mount Zion (14:1–5) can only be realized by one who has felt the chilling terror inspired by the "beast rising out of the sea" (13:1) and the "beast which rose out of the earth" (13:11–18). And the joy attending the descent of the New Jerusalem, "prepared as a bride adorned for her husband" (21:2), takes on a different dimension as it is seen against the confusion and chaos resulting from the fall of the earthly city, Babylon (18:1–24).

Exploring the many emotional impacts of Revelation, and especially the sharp alternations of despair and hope, fear and courage, gloom and ecstatic happiness, can be a useful approach to the message of the book. Not only does it allow us to enter into the events that are described, but it points to the heart of John's message: the great conflict in which no one can remain uncommitted.

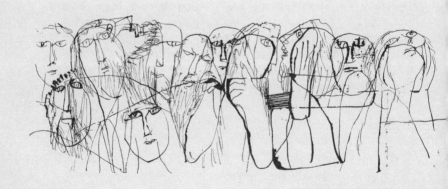

When this was done I looked again, and before my
eyes appeared a vast crowd beyond man's power to number. They came from every nation and tribe and people
and language, and they stood before the throne of the
Lamb, dressed in white robes with palm branches in
their hands. With a great voice they shouted these words:
"Salvation belongs to our God who sits upon the throne
and to the Lamb!"

Then all the angels stood encircling the throne, the
elders and the four living creatures, and prostrated themselves with heads bowed before the throne and worshiped
God saying,

"Amen! Blessing and glory and wisdom and thanks-
giving and honor and power and strength be given to
our God for timeless ages!"

Then one of the elders addressed me and asked,

"These who are dressed in white robes—who are they,
and where do they come from?"

"You know, my Lord," I answered him.

Then he told me:

"These are those who have come through the great
oppression; they have washed their robes and made
them white in the blood of the Lamb. That is why they
now have their place before the throne of God, and serve
him day and night in his temple. He who sits upon the
throne will be their shelter. They will never again know
hunger or thirst. The sun shall never beat upon them,
neither shall there be any scorching heat, for the Lamb
who is in the center of the throne will be their shepherd
and will lead them to springs of living water. And God
will wipe away every tear from their eyes."

REVELATION 7:9–17
J. B. Phillips translation

9 · The Symbolism of Revelation

A SYMBOL is anything used to convey something other than the "face value" of the symbol itself. A familiar symbol that illustrates this is the flag of your country or the pennant of your favorite baseball team. By itself the flag is only a rectangular piece of cloth with certain colors and geometric patterns. But it represents a great deal more. It reminds us of the past history of our country, of heroic deeds and great moments when our destiny was at stake. It stands also for the authority and the prestige of our nation at the present, and it speaks of our unity as a people with a common allegiance. These deeper meanings of the flag are the reason why we have elaborate rules as to how the flag is displayed, how to handle it when it is hoisted or taken down, and even how to dispose of it when it has become worn out. These rules would be quite ridiculous if the flag were nothing more than a piece of cloth.

All kinds of physical objects can become symbols. The central Christian symbol, the cross, is in its simplest form just two pieces of wood nailed together—not unlike the telephone poles that we see along country roads. But for the devout Christian this symbol speaks eloquently of the things that matter most in his life: of suffering love, of redemption and hope, and of victory over sin. It matters little what the cross symbol is made of: the "old rugged cross" that inspired the writing of the hymn of that name or the jeweler's creation of gold and precious stones both tell essentially the same story. A symbol of death has become a symbol of life.

Symbolic Words

Words can also be symbols. The word "constitution" brings to our mind not only a document that was written nearly two hundred years ago, but something precious that must be guarded against all infringements. The ancient Hebrews thought that the name for God was so holy that they did not dare pronounce it, and substituted another name when they read the Bible. In this case, too, the name meant much more than the combination of letters used to identify God.

The symbolic use of words gives richness and depth to our language and helps us to communicate many things that would be impossible to convey if we were limited to drab factual statements. Two of the simplest and most common ways in which we use words symbolically are through similes and metaphors. And we find as we read the Bible that both of these are used often and effectively.

Similes

A simile is a comparison between two objects that differ in most respects but still may be alike in some way that is important to the writer's purpose. It says specifically that one is like the other, using the word "like" or "as." An example of a biblical simile is found in Psalm 1, in the statement that the God-fearing man is "like a tree planted by streams of water." Here the writer suggests that there is a parallel between a pious man and a tree growing in a place where it will never suffer from drought. He could, of course, have said that the pious man will always have an adequate life, but the simile is a much more vivid and fresh way of expressing this important idea.

Metaphors

A metaphor is much like a simile in that it compares two items, but the comparison is implied rather than stated explicitly. An example of a bibical metaphor is found in the well-known phrase from Psalm 23: "The LORD is my shepherd." This statement does not mean that the Lord is literally a shepherd and that those who trust in him are literally sheep. But it does suggest something significant about the relationship between God and those who believe in him; and for those who are at all familiar with sheep and the way they are cared for by a good shepherd, this metaphor can convey more than a thousand words in plain, factual language.

Parables

Similes and metaphors are often single words or short phrases, and there are more elaborate ways in which words can be used symbolically to express meaning that is not apparent on the surface. One example of this is the parable, a teaching method that was used often by Christ. The parable tells a story, usually from ordinary life, but points out a spiritual truth that goes far beyond the immediate meaning of the story.

The parable of the woman who lost a silver coin and went through the house with light and broom, searching until she found it (Luke 15:8–10), pictures a thoroughly familiar and credible situation. It could happen in any place and at any time, and one can easily sense the worry of the woman and her sense of relief and happiness when she found the missing coin. But a magnificent new dimension is added to this story when we realize that this is how God feels about a human being who is lost in sin and then is found. To get the full impact of this message we must get more than the abstract idea that God cares for the sinner. We must sense the feeling that is involved, and a parable can convey this feeling much better than a factual discussion.

Another important characteristic of the parable is its emphasis on one central truth. Details of the story simply aid in bringing out this main message.

Allegories

The allegory differs from the parable in that each part has a special meaning. For instance, Christ's description of himself as the true vine and his followers as the branches (John 15:1 ff.) is an allegory rather than a parable, and it is quite proper to look for the meaning of each part in this picture. But there is a rather limited use of allegories in the Bible. Nothing but confusion and error will result if we try to give allegorical meaning to stories or other passages in the Bible that were not meant to be understood this way. For example, there is no point in looking for special meaning in the oil and wine that the Good Samaritan poured on the wounds of the man who had been mistreated by the robbers (Luke 10:34). Oil and wine were simply a common first-aid treatment at that time, and this part of the story merely shows that the Samaritan did everything he could to help the unfortunate victim and in this way demonstrated what it means to love one's neighbor whoever he happens to be.

Fables and Myths

There are two other ways in which spiritual meaning is expressed in symbolic form—the fable and the myth. The fable, like the parable, tells a story, but its story differs markedly from the everyday story of the parable. In the fable very unusual things happen. A biblical example of a fable is found in the story of the different trees talking to each other and trying to elect one of their company as their king (Judges 9:7–15). No one, including the author who wrote this passage, would argue that the trees actually did talk and decided to elect the bramble as their king. But the lesson of this fable is quite meaningful, for it relates to the problems that the people of Israel were facing at the time, and the lesson is effectively expressed in this form.

While the fable is usually concerned with a limited problem, the myth deals with large universal themes involving not only man but also divine and demonic beings. For instance, virtually all religions in the world have myths that attempt to

85

REVELATION 16:13–14

show how man and the world came into existence and why life is the way it is. Important institutions, such as marriage and the family and royalty, are also frequently justified or explained by means of myths.

The reader who has accepted without qualms the use of similes, metaphors, parables, allegories, and even fables in the Bible, may hesitate at the thought of calling anything in the Bible a myth. The reason for this hesitation is simple. In ordinary English usage, the word "myth" is often used to signify something that is the opposite of truth or, even worse, to foster an illusion that is both false and misleading. However, as Webster points out, the meaning of the term "myth" is "a usually traditional story of ostensibly historical events that serves to unfold part of the world view of a people or explain a practice, belief, or natural phenomenon."

When the word "myth" is used in this way, it describes stories or accounts that deal with the large and important subjects of human experience in the same way in which the parable tells a story to illustrate a spiritual truth. In this sense of the word, it is proper to call the Creation Story in Genesis a myth. This is to say that the Creation Story in Genesis should not be understood as a scientific account of how this world and man came into being—the kind of account that a physicist and a biologist would attempt to give. The Genesis story shows, as a parable would, a meaning that is not apparent on the surface, that this world and all that is in it owe their existence to God's creative and sustaining power.

Something in Common

These various ways words are used as symbols differ in some respects, but they all have something in common—they point to a meaning other than that which is apparent on the surface. Thus these symbolic forms have a power that ordinary, factual language seldom achieves. They appeal not only to the intellect but to the feelings and imagination. None of these symbolic forms of communication, including the parables that Christ liked to use, are in themselves religious forms of speech.

87

All can be used for nonreligious purposes as well. They become religious symbols when they are used to express meanings that pertain specifically to the spiritual life. Some contemporary writers point out that the symbolic form of communication is uniquely suited to deal with matters pertaining to the spiritual life because there is so much in the spiritual world that eludes our ordinary, prosaic thought forms. It is not surprising, therefore, that the Bible—from the first book to the last—makes such prodigious use of symbolism.

John's Word Symbols

As you have noticed in your reading, John made extensive use of symbolism in his writing of Revelation. It is important, therefore, to understand what kinds of symbolism John used, for this will often be decisive in our attempt to interpret the meaning of his writing. As we compare the writing of John with the various types of word symbolism we have examined, it seems clear that he uses myths more than any of the others. He deals with large universal themes that involve not only man but also divine and demonic beings.

But it would be unwise to try to classify John's book in a rigid manner. He also uses an abundance of similes and metaphors, and even has a number of frankly allegorical features. For instance, the "sharp two-edged sword" (1:16) that issued from the mouth of the exalted Christ in John's initial vision is obviously an allegorical symbol for the Word of God. And the ten horns, seven heads, and ten diadems of the beast (13:1) are also allegorical symbols.

John's writing also differs from most myths in its wealth of detail. In his further description of the beast that rose out of the sea he speaks about it being like a leopard, with feet like a bear's and a mouth like that of a lion. These features may be allegorical and serve the purpose of similes—combining the characteristics of the three ferocious animals, each noted for its strength and wildness. Likewise, in his description of the rider on the white horse (19:11–16), John uses many details that may be partly allegorical and partly metaphorical, the total effect of which is a powerful picture of the invincible Christ who will conquer the nations of the world and "rule them with a rod of iron." This attention to detail seems to be common in apocalyptic literature, as we can see in the writings of Ezekiel (see 10:1–22). But it forms a rather sharp contrast to the simplicity of the Creation Story in Genesis.

Revelation and other apocalyptic writings differ in their use of religious myths in another important respect. Most of these myths are concerned with the origin of things and seek to explain things as they are now in terms of something that happened in the past. Their orientation is retrospective. John, on the other hand, looks toward the future and the ultimate goal toward which all things are moving. He seeks to explain things as they are now in terms of what will come to pass.

The theological term used to describe this concern with the future and the ultimate goal of all things is "eschatology," which is derived from a Greek word that means "farthest" or "the last in a series" and hence is used to refer to the end of the world and "last things." If we use this word and call John's seven visions of the future "eschatological myths," we may have the best possible description of both Revelation and other apocalyptic writings in the Bible.

When we call the visions of John eschatological myths, it does *not* mean that John's visions of the future are meaningless fantasies that have no bearing on the real world. What it does mean is that we ought not to expect that the dramatic events in John's seven visions will literally take place; they are not and never will become historical events in the same sense that the Battle of Waterloo and the bombing of Pearl Harbor are historical events. They describe in a symbolic manner the inner dynamics of historical events, the continual struggle between good and evil with the eventual triumph of good. This means that we must be careful to interpret the visions of John in such a way that we never lose sight of their symbolic and mythological character.

10 · The Message of the Symbols

O SAY that John's seven visions of the future do not describe events that will actually take place may seem to some people like an attempt to give an interpretation to Revelation that John himself did not intend. There is in the book, for instance, the often-repeated statement that the visions were given John so that he could show the church "what must soon take place." And in the concluding part of the book, this statement is followed by the warning "Behold, I am coming soon" (22:7), to which the church responds "Amen. Come, Lord Jesus!" (22:20).

Current Events

We notice also that there are a great number of references, both direct and veiled, in John's writing to conditions and situations that existed in his own time. He speaks about the people of Israel, even mentioning each of the twelve tribes by name (7:1–8). The people of Israel is also the symbolic meaning of the woman who gave birth to a child and fled to the wilderness (12:1 ff.). The beast that rose out of the sea is clearly a symbol for the Roman Empire (13:1–10), and the beast that rose out of the earth refers undoubtedly to the

THE MESSAGE OF THE SYMBOLS

practice of emperor worship (13:11–18). Nearly all Bible scholars agree that the mystic number 666 (13:18) is a numerical code for Nero, the emperor who died in A.D. 68 but who was expected by many Christians to rise again and become the marshal of all evil forces.

Geographical names like Mount Zion (14:1) and the river Euphrates (16:12) are easily identified as the site of Jerusalem and one of the great rivers in ancient Babylonia. Armageddon, the gathering place for the final battle of the kings of the world (16:16), is identified as a famous old battleground in Palestine, on the plains just south of Nazareth. The Babylon whose fall is described in the eighteenth chapter is clearly a symbol for ancient Rome, and Rome is also the intended meaning of the mother of harlots who is described in the seventeenth chapter. The Gog and Magog who are to fight in the final battle (20:7–10) cannot be readily identified, but these names were apparently used by John—as they were used by Ezekiel before him (see Ezekiel 39:1)—to symbolize brutal and inhuman military forces in much the same way people later spoke of the Huns and the Tartars.

Failure or Fact?

All these references to places and conditions in the world that John saw before him at the end of the first century seem to suggest that if he was so clear about current references then his visions of what "must soon take place" were meant to describe specific historical events. But if this is the correct interpretation of Revelation, then we have to admit that most of John's visions of the future did not come to pass. There has been no dearth of trouble and unhappiness in the world since the prophet of Patmos wrote his book, but nothing has happened that we can honestly say is like that which John describes in his seven visions of the future. This would mean that John's book misled its earliest readers and has no message that is truly relevant to our situation now. (This may well be one major reason why many contemporary Christians have simply ignored Revelation.)

91

But there is still another possibility which has been the position of many people who still maintain that John described real historical events. This view admits that the word "soon" in the statement "what must soon take place" should not be understood literally. They suggest that there is a kind of telescoping of time in John's perspective, so that what is still far off may seem close at hand. According to this, John describes real historical events, but they have not yet come to pass. They will occur, however, at the end of time, at some unknown date in the future. But even this is difficult to envision, for a number of reasons.

John's Limited View

It is by no means improbable that life here on earth may come to an end someday. A variety of astronomical cataclysms could bring this about. The sudden explosion of stars in other parts of the universe has been observed more than once; it is not impossible that the same thing could happen to our sun. Even a man-made nuclear holocaust could snuff out all life on earth. And John's vision of the seven trumpets (8:7—9:21) seems to involve a great many astronomical and other natural phenomena.

That the real end of the world will occur the way John's visions suggest if they are interpreted literally, is more than difficult to envision. For one thing, John's perspective of the world is a rather limited one, both geographically and scientifically. His geographical world was limited to the countries surrounding the Mediterranean Sea. And although he speaks about people "from every nation, from all tribes and peoples and tongues" (7:9), there is nothing in his book to suggest that he was aware of a world that extended north of the Alps, across the Atlantic, south of the Sahara, and to the Far East. It is also impossible to reconcile the natural disasters described by John in his vision of the seven trumpets with the knowledge we have today of the earth and outer space.

Furthermore, if John's visions of the future describe historical events that are yet to take place, they show a disturbing lack of awareness of technological developments and other changes that have already taken place and will doubtless continue to take place in the future. His wars are still fought on horseback, and the sword is the main weapon. The inventory of goods for which the merchants of the fallen Babylon could no longer find customers (18:11–13) looks rather slim when it is compared with what is sold in cities today. To be sure, there are some interpreters of Revelation who have tried to find hints of modern inventions in the book. For instance, they have suggested that the locust that could sting like a scorpion (9:3–11) symbolizes modern war weapons. But this kind of allegorization is more clever than honest.

These considerations seem to leave only two alternatives: either to dismiss John's visions of the future as a kind of dream that has no real bearing on the world as we know it, or else to give some serious consideration to regarding John's visions of the future as eschatological myths.

An Artistic Example

To interpret these visions as eschatological myths means first of all to make a clear distinction between the symbolic material through which meaning is expressed and the meaning itself. This should be done, of course, in all cases where the meaning of symbolic representation is studied, including objects of art. And it may be helpful here to examine the way in which an artist makes use of symbolic material in order to express his meaning.

A painting by the sixteenth-century artist El Greco, "Agony in the Garden," deals with Christ's experience in Gethsemane before his crucifixion. In the background of this picture we can see the foreboding sky and the somber landscape that appear in other paintings by El Greco, such as his "Storm over Toledo." The elongated figure of Christ in the foreground wears the traditional red robe, but Christ has a distinctly Spanish face. The position of his body suggests one who is kneeling but is about to stand up, so that we are not allowed to think that this position is a permanent one. The indistinct figures of the sleeping disciples are arranged in a way that may suggest unborn fetuses in a womb. The angel that is hovering between heaven and earth radiates masculine strength, but Christ's look seems to be directed upward and beyond him. And the distant figures of those who are coming to arrest Christ seem to be merely variations in the foreboding landscape.

The paint and canvas that El Greco used in painting this picture comprise his medium, just as John's medium is his language. El Greco's materials are first of all the New Testament story about Christ's agonizing prayer in Gethsemane. But included among his materials are also many elements from the artist's own environment, so that the picture as a whole looks more like El Greco's sixteenth-century Spain than first-century Jerusalem.

A naïve critic of El Greco's painting might say that the artist has made a mistake in putting Christ in a Spanish landscape, and especially in giving Christ the face of a Spanish nobleman. He might also point to anatomical faults, both in the elongated figure of Christ and in the other figures that are depicted. He might thus dismiss El Greco as a rather inept painter who should go back to his drawing lessons before undertaking another picture.

But a more perceptive study of "Agony in the Garden" will show that the artist is far from being a clumsy novice in his painterly skills.

Materials Shape the Message

El Greco's subtle use of materials from both the New Testament and his own environment, and especially the Spanish face of Christ, is a powerful way of saying in a symbolic way that his purpose is not just to picture an event that happened many centuries ago but to point to a timeless and universal meaning. The excruciating agony of having to weigh the will to live one's own life against the surrender of oneself to "thy will be done" is not an isolated historical incident but an eternal problem, equally relevant to El Greco's sixteenth-century Spain and to our twentieth century. Even the anatomical distortions and the other improbable elements in El Greco's painting serve to give emphasis to this meaning. A painting which tried to reproduce the original scene with photographic accuracy would most likely fail to get this message across.

Like El Greco, John used materials that were at hand in his own environment. We see reflected in his writing the immediate problems of the church coming face to face with persecution. We see the threatening aspects of the Roman Empire, its vast powers organized in the service of evil. We see also much evidence of disruptive forces at work within this empire, for even in the first century the Roman Empire was experiencing many of the troubles that were to bring about its downfall a few centuries later. In addition to this, we can find among John's materials much that he has adopted from Ezekiel, Daniel, and other apocalpytic writers. And last but not least, there is John's central conviction that the exalted Christ is not only the lord of the church but the lord of the world and of history. All these elements help determine both the form and meaning of his book.

The Timeless Meaning

The distinction between symbolic material and meaning calls attention to the fact that while the form in which the meaning is given may be "dated," the meaning itself may be timeless. If the Parable of the Good Samaritan were told now, it might well speak of travel in a jet airliner rather than a journey on foot down a deserted wilderness road. But the message of the parable, to "love your neighbor as yourself," would be just as meaningful and relevant. We understand and appreciate the message of this parable even now because we do realize that the meaning of the message is not to be confused with the form in which it was originally given.

The great value of symbolic representation is not only that in this way we can suggest things that are virtually impossible to express in ordinary, factual language. Even more important is the fact that the connection between the symbolic material and the meaning remains loose enough so that the two can be distinguished. This is not the case with factual statements. For example, Paul's rather adamant statement "I permit no woman to teach or to have authority over men; she is to keep silent" (1 Timothy 2:12) does reflect the social and cultural conditions of his own times, and was probably a good rule under those conditions. But what can we do with a statement like this now? There seem to be only two alternatives: either we accept it or we reject it. The parables of Christ do not confront us with this kind of dilemma. Although most of them reflect a rural and ancient form of life that is far removed from our metropolitan kind of existence, their meaning is just as relevant as it was two thousand years ago.

Use of the Past

The chief problem with symbolic representation is that the symbols may lose their power; in other words, they may be so remote from our present mode of existence that they no longer can engage our imagination. We tend to take a great deal of pride in being up-to-date in our knowledge, in the furnishing of our homes, and in our general outlook on life. This attitude often goes hand in hand with a tendency to depreciate anything that is identified with earlier ages and modes of life. In this frame of mind we may look at John's beast arising out of the sea, or even the rider on the white horse, as something quaint and anachronistic that has no real meaning or relevance for us.

Many things suggest that our ties with the past are far stronger than we often suspect. Primitive cave paintings more than 10,000 years old can make a profound impression on modern people. Drumbeats from the African forest can excite sophisticated citizens in a modern metropolis. Ancient sculptures and wood carvings are proudly exhibited in strictly contemporary living rooms. Modern scholars spend a lifetime studying the remains of cultures that vanished a long time ago. Historical novels dealing with the remote past hit the best-seller list. Even if symbols that were once powerful expressions of meaning seem to have lost most of their power, it may be that

REVELATION 17:3–5

the power is still latently present and only needs to be redis-covered. Just as we try to translate the words of the Bible from Hebrew and Greek into modern English, so we need to re-capture the power of the symbols that are used in the Bible. Perhaps we even need to explore translating biblical symbols into current symbols that better convey truth to modern man.

John's Main Point

As we approach John's visions of the future in this way, we acknowledge that they are eschatological myths expressing, in terms relevant to his time, meanings that have eternal significance. This means we must recognize that although the symbolic material in Revelation comes from John's own century and refers to conditions and situations that existed then, he is not merely speaking about the Roman Empire or any other particular nation at any other time in history. John's message is concerned with any and all attempts by human beings to find the meaning of their existence and organize their activities and purposes apart from fellowship with God. For John, the Roman Empire was the epitome of this attempt. For other people in other ages it may be some other empire, or it may have nothing at all to do with a particular political structure. It may just as soon be some other human organization, such as a teenage gang, the home community, a business concern, an educational institution, a family.

The basic message of Revelation in this regard is that no attempt to organize a society of human beings apart from fellow-ship with God can lead to anything except enmity toward God. There is no middle ground or neutral position. There is only Babylon versus the New Jerusalem, the kingdom of men versus the kingdom of God. This means also that hostility between the two is inevitable. There can be no peace on earth so long as the two kingdoms exist side by side. The kingdom of men will seek to destroy the kingdom of God, and the kingdom of God will seek to conquer the kingdom of men. Then, in addition, the kingdom of men suffers from internal conflicts that help to bring about its destruction.

Emphasis on Groups

It may be well to point out here that apart from a modest role John himself plays as the recorder of the visions and the strong figure of Christ, there is no individual personality that stands out and comes to life in the Book of Revelation. The messages to the seven churches are addressed to congregations rather than individuals, and it is the church in Laodicea rather than particular members that Christ threatens to spew out of his mouth. We hear about multitudes that sing the new song of praise to the Lamb, but they are virtually faceless in their ecstatic joy. We hear about the kings of the earth, about great men and generals and slaves and freemen and merchants, but none of them is seen as a distinct individual. Even the reference to Nero is veiled and obscure. And there is no mention of the great biblical heroes of faith—Abraham, Moses, Elijah, or Paul—in the visionary views of heaven.

The most plausible explanation for this preoccupation with groups rather than with individual human beings is that John is looking at things from a great distance in much the same way we look at a distant mountain and find that the crags and crevices disappear and only the broad outlines stand out. But to this may be added another thought: From John's point of view, human existence is not a matter of each individual finding his own way through life and then harvesting the consequences of his actions. We are members of a community, the church, the people of God. We can become either the community of the redeemed or the community of those who revolt against God. John's primary purpose is to show what happens to these two communities, both as they confront each other in this world and in terms of their ultimate destiny.

11 · The Pattern of the Visions

LET'S take a closer look at John's seven visions of the future and explore their rich significance. We will deal with hints for further thought rather than cut-and-dried, detailed explanations. We do not want the imposition of a rigid set of explanations—we profit more in our study of Revelation if we let the symbolic material stimulate our imagination and provoke our thoughts.

Preliminaries

Chapters 4 and 5 are preliminary to the visions that follow in the same way that John's initial vision of the exalted Christ (1:9–20) is a preliminary to the messages to the seven churches. The report of what John saw when he entered heaven "in the Spirit" (4:2) serves to establish the perspective on all that is to follow. John describes God as "one seated on the throne" in a glory that can be depicted only by metaphorical reference to precious stones. This and his account of the adoration of God by those who surround the throne leave the reader no room for doubt about who is the ruler of the universe. As the creator of all things, by whose will all things exist (4:11), God's place on the throne remains secure; and at no time during the turmoil of the following visions is his sovereignty threatened.

This section serves also to establish the role of Christ as the one whose hands set in motion and keep control over unfolding events in the earthly realm. The seven horns and the seven eyes of the Lamb symbolize his complete authority, his omnipotence and omnipresence in the world. The scroll with its seven seals, a symbol which may have been borrowed from the Old Testament (see Ezekiel 2:9–10), represents the future that is about to be revealed. And John adds that the authority of Christ in his role as the lord of the world and the lord of history is acknowledged by all creation (5:13).

A Vision of Destruction

As the perspective shifts from this heavenly vantage point to the earth in the first of the seven visions of the future (6:1—7:17), there is a dramatic change of atmosphere. Instead of glory and praise around the heavenly throne we see a world teeming with trouble. The four horsemen (6:2–8), a symbol probably borrowed from the Old Testament (see Zechariah 1:8; 6:1–8), represent the breakdown of human civilization through militarism, civil strife, famine, and other destructive agents. The fifth seal (6:9–11) reveals persecution of those who are faithful to the Word of God, while the sixth seal indicates drastic physical disturbances on earth (6:12–14) and a loss of nerve among the inhabitants on earth (6:15–17).

The reader might well pause here and inquire: What does this have to do with the lordship of Christ as the redeemer of the world? Is the disintegration of human civilization and of the world itself the purpose of history? Does God delight in destroying that which he has created? Questions like these are by no means irreverent, and they are necessary.

Love and Wrath

The paradoxical phrase "the wrath of the Lamb" (6:16) may provide the clue we need to find the answers to these questions. There is a kind of wrath which is motivated by hostility, hatred, or complete rejection of others; and such a wrath is utterly destructive. But the lamb image in the Bible never symbolizes these attitudes. The lamb is gentle and patient, a friendly animal that is not given to vicious attacks. And the Lamb of God is the supreme symbol of the sacrificial love of God for this world, as is clearly indicated in the song of the twenty-four elders: ". . . Thou wast slain and by thy blood didst ransom men for God" (5:9). What, then, can "the wrath of the Lamb" mean?

The conjunction of love and wrath, suggested by the elders' song, does indeed dispel a certain sentimental concept of love in which the whole emphasis is upon the benign and permissive attitude of the lover. Such a sentimental kind of love is without much character and depth. The love of God for man is not like this: God does not overlook the faults of man, but in his love he offers remedies for these faults, and this is exactly what the Lamb represents—God's loving answer to man's sinfulness. The Lamb is the symbol of redemption, and "the wrath of the Lamb" can mean only one thing, namely, that redemption has been rejected by man.

Life Without Christ

The world pictured by John in his first vision of the future is one in which the Lamb has been rejected. The disintegration of both human civilization and physical aspects is the result of this rejection. Human life without the redeeming power of Christ is self-defeating, and any society from which this power is excluded will disintegrate. The four horsemen riding through the world scattering trouble are a vivid symbol of this fundamental fact about existence. And the panic among the citizens of a world in which the Lamb has been rejected is another vivid image of the futility and ultimate disruption of a civilization so conceived. These are the people who become aware of "the wrath of the Lamb."

However, this world is not without some people who have remained faithful to the Word of God, even at the cost of

102

martyrdom (6:9). There is a direct line from Israel to the Christian church in John's thinking. John's meticulous naming of the twelve tribes of Israel (7:4–8) is no doubt meant to bring to mind the idea of the chosen people. The number of the redeemed from every tribe clearly has symbolic meaning. It is interesting to note that the prime factors of twelve, when added together, give the number seven (3 + 2 + 2 = 7). The number 1000 is generally used in the Bible to indicate a large but indefinite number (see Psalm 90:4). Thus, 12 x 12 x 1000 gives 144,000, the number of the redeemed. This symbolic number suggests that in spite of the world's rejection of the Lamb there will be a large number of people who are in harmony with God's redemptive plan. That John here does not think just of the actual descendants of Abraham but of all those who are truly members of the church is made clear in the following passage (7:9–17). The criterion for membership in the chosen people is that "they have washed their robes and made them white in the blood of the Lamb" (7:14).

Setting the Pattern

John's first vision thus sets the pattern for everything that follows. On the one hand, there is the host of those who reject the Lamb and will ultimately discover that their way of life has been a colossal mistake. Then there are those who have accepted the Lamb, who have the seal of God upon their foreheads (7:3). Their lot is not always an easy one here on earth, but they are nevertheless the inheritors of the future. The perspective of John's first vision reaches all the way to eternity, to the great fulfillment that will come when God, in the words of Paul, "may be everything to every one" (1 Corinthians 15:28). This perspective is what gives meaning and purpose to the followers of the Lamb here on earth.

Understood in this way, John's first vision does not point to any particular period in history, and it does not describe any particular set of events in the near or distant future. Rather, it speaks of the situation in all historical periods. The description of the natural catastrophes (6:12–14) is not

REVELATION 19:21

to be regarded as a preview of the end of the world, but is a vivid way of saying that even nature itself will not sustain those who reject God's redemption in Christ.

Trumpets and Prayers

The breaking of the seventh seal (8:1) is the end of the first vision; but it is also the beginning of the next vision, and this seems to be John's subtle way of saying that this vision is to be understood as a restatement or elaboration of what was revealed in the first vision. The "silence in heaven for about half an hour" that follows immediately after the breaking of the seal can mean a great many things, but above all it serves to focus attention on what is about to be revealed. The introduction of the seven episodes in the next vision by trumpet blasts lends additional emphasis to the importance of what is about to happen. In the Old Testament, the sound of the trumpet is often used as a symbol of God's intervention in the affairs of man (see Isaiah 27:12–13).

The little interlude dealing with "the prayers of all the saints" (8:3–5) calls attention to the fact that the fate of the chosen people or the redeemed is a major concern in all that is about to happen. Their prayers, mixed with heavenly incense and returned to earth, create the thunderous prelude to the sounding of the seven trumpets. There could hardly be a more effective way of showing that Christian prayers are not in vain.

Nature Without God

The first four trumpet blasts call forth various kinds of physical disasters (8:7–12). It would be both impossible and pointless to attempt to explain these phenomena as natural events that will take place someday. For one thing, John's description of these disasters assumes the view, common in his day, that the earth is flat and that the sky above is like an inverted bowl whose perimeter contains all the heavenly bodies. It is far more helpful to recall that in the Old Testament natural disasters are usually understood to be the consequence of disobedience and rebellion against God. This was the reason for the great flood in Noah's time, and why Sodom and Gomorrah were buried in a rain of brimstone and fire. The ten plagues that befell Pharaoh and the Egyptians, in many respects similar to what John describes in his second vision, came because they refused to heed God's command to let the people of Israel go.

The deeper meaning of this kind of thinking is not difficult to understand. Those who rebel against God and try to find the meaning of their existence apart from God always end up trying to make this earth their permanent home and turning to the physical world for the meaning of their existence. This earth and all of nature are God's creation; but when they are used in this way, as the basis for rebellion against God, they become threats to man's existence. Nature without God offers man no security, and those who put their trust in the things of this world will find that there is nothing they can depend on. These are inevitable consequences when, as Paul puts it, man serves the creature rather than the Creator (see Romans 1:18–32).

Despair and Terror

To these physical disasters, the fifth and sixth trumpets (9:1–21) add demonic terrors that emerge from "the bottomless pit" (9:2). Not only does nature fail to support those who have turned away from God, but human existence becomes exposed to demonic powers. There is a fascinating but frightening description of the appearance of the locusts (9:7–11), whose "faces were like human faces." And the image of two-hundred million horsemen with deathly power roaming the earth (9:13–19) adds to the horror. It becomes clear that one of John's chief aims in this vision is to describe the brutal despair and horror of human existence apart from God.

But in what way is John's description relevant to our lives? And, furthermore, what does it have to do with the role of Christ as the redeemer of the world? The despair that can grip human life in alienation from God is no less frightful than

John's vivid visions of physical chaos and demonic destruction. The experience of Luther in the years before he discovered the meaning of faith bears this out. And countless others have also known this despair. This is not to say that every human being lives in fear and trembling until he has made his peace with God. But the nightmarish quality of John's visions suggests the possibility that every human being feels the emotions that find expression in John's imagery.

This leads us to another consideration of Christ as our redeemer. Redemption does not become a personal experience until the individual has become aware of his need for redemption. In this sense "the wrath of the Lamb" is the first expression of his love, for it prepares the way for repentance and fellowship with him. Judgment of the sinner goes hand in hand with his justification. But it should be noted, as John also makes clear (9:20–21), that the disintegration of life away from God does not automatically lead to the experience of redemption.

Interlude

Chapter 10 and the first fourteen verses of Chapter 11 form a kind of interlude in the unfolding of the main visions. The first part of this section (10:1–11) alludes enigmatically to "a little scroll' or a separate revelation that John is not permitted to disclose but later is told to eat, finding it sweet to his taste but indigestible. The seven thunders that give voice to this revelation suggest that the content has to do with the same message that is expressed in the other visions. What is this "mystery of God" (10:7) that must remain a secret?

Perhaps what John intends to convey in this passage is mainly what is expressed in William Cowper's hymn: "God moves in a mysterious way His wonders to perform." That is to say: we should never think that we know the whole story of what is happening in the world. God has resources and plans that are beyond human understanding. In a science-centered society this human inability to explain the methods of God often causes frustration. This need not be so.

Church and Covenant

The last part of this section (11:1–14) is probably best understood as an anticipation of the next main vision. The temple that John is asked to measure (11:1–3) seems to suggest the church, the new community of the people of God that is God's answer to the society of godless men. And the beast that "ascends from the bottomless pit" (11:7) is the symbol of this godless society that will fight against God's new community.

The blowing of the seventh trumpet is followed by a little interlude quite similar to the one after the opening of the seventh seal, and here the exposure of the Ark of the Covenant —clearly a symbol of the church—brings about the same dramatic sound effects that in the earlier passage were associated with the prayers of the saints. These are John's subtle ways of suggesting that the next vision is again to be an elaboration of the message of the previous visions.

Vision of Conflict

The now-familiar system of dividing each main vision into seven parts is not so easily discernible in the next vision (12:1—14:20), but it is not impossible to find seven distinct parts here also. It is important to notice that if the secret vision of the seven thunders is counted as the third vision, which John seems to have intended, the vision now under consideration is the fourth in the series; and, as was intimated earlier, the number four has a pivotal place in a series of seven. This may also be hinted at in John's statement about the importance of the seventh trumpet (10:7), which signals the beginning of the new vision. That is to say: the main answer to the problem of a world in rebellion against God is to be introduced in this vision.

The Greek word used to describe this vision, *semeion* (translated "portent") is the same word that is used in the Gospel of John as a name for the acts by which Christ "manifested his glory" (John 2:11). Some scholars believe that the "woman clothed with the sun, with the moon under her feet, and on her head a crown of twelve stars" (12:1), and also the great dragon with its sweeping tail (12:3–4), are astrological symbols; if so, this may be John's way of suggesting the universal significance of these images. The woman is obviously a symbol of the Hebrew nation in its role as a chosen people, and the son to whom the woman gave birth can be none other than Christ. And the great red dragon suggests the Roman Empire, which for John was the epitome of man's rebellion against God. The reference to the ascension of Christ and the scattering of the Hebrew nation after the destruction of Jerusalem in A.D.70 (12:5–6) makes this interpretation quite conclusive.

John's purpose in this vision is, first of all, to point to Christ as God's remedy for the predicament of sin. But he also wants to show where the battle line is to be drawn: between the community of the redeemed and the society of the world. The battle is not just an episode here on earth but involves the whole universe (12:7–17), and the opposition to Christ and his followers is crystallized into a conscious and powerful movement with strong leadership (13:1–18). Each person is marked, either by the "name of the beast" (13:17) or by the "Father's name" (14:1). There is no middle ground for those who would like to remain uncommitted.

The position of Christ's followers appears to be insecure in this conflict, but the rest of the vision (14:1–20) points to their victory in the final outcome.

This vision ends with another intimation that the society of men will disintegrate, and this is the theme returned to in the next vision (15:1—16:21). Here the division into seven parts, in the form of seven bowls of wrath, is again clear; and the content of this vision is very much like that of the vision of the seven trumpets.

Dramatic Downfall

The last of the seven visions of the future (17:1—20:15) begins with a description of the evils of the society of men (17:1–18), but then moves on to a dramatic account of the downfall of this society (18:1–24). The triumph of the Lamb takes the form of a defeat of the nations and an ultimate victory over all demonic powers (19:1—20:10). Included in this triumph is the vision that all living souls as well as those who have died must account for their own role in the universal struggle (20:11–15).

Postlude

The last part of John's account is related to the visions of the future in much the same way as his initial vision of heaven (4:1 ff.). In that vision he saw what could be called the "prelude" to the visions. In the last part of Revelation (21:1—22:5), he is watching the postlude. In the first part of the vision he was transported from a troubled earth into heaven for a look behind the scenes; here heaven is coming down to earth, and all troubles have disappeared. There is a quietness about this scene, much like when a hurricane has finally blown itself out and the first chirp of a bird is heard again. The city of men has been destroyed and even its ruins have vanished; but the city of God is now descending to take its place.

No wonder Christians found in this image of the New Jerusalem the focus of their hope for life after death. And as a symbol of the ultimate victory in Christ over both sin and death, nothing could be more appropriate. To interpret John's visions as eschatological myths is to note that his New Jerusalem is also related to life here on earth now. The designation of the New Jerusalem as "the Bride, the wife of the Lamb" (21:9) provides a clue. The New Jerusalem is John's vision of the church and its potentialities as a community of the redeemed people of God. This is a vision of the church that will quell forever the smug self-satisfaction of Laodicea and all her sister congregations throughout the ages. And it may also contain the final explanation of the paradoxical statement that the poor and troubled church of Smyrna is nevertheless rich.

Here John gives us a breathtaking view of the potentialities of the church as the new community in this world. The New

Jerusalem is not just a remote possibility in a far-distant future but a real encounter with the living Christ within the fellowship of the church here and now. Our experience of this new community may be fragmentary and sporadic, but if it occurs the result will always be a heightened sense of expectancy and a sense of personal fulfillment through participation in the life of the church.

12 · The Society of Men

OUR examination of the message of Revelation has brought out two things we should note carefully. One is John's habit of referring to groups rather than individuals. The other is the sharp battle line he draws between the group of men called society and the group of men called the community of the redeemed. Both of these ideas, and especially the latter, can easily be misunderstood and can lead to erroneous conclusions far removed from John's meaning and the whole tenor of the biblical message.

Church and Society

One example of the kind of misunderstanding that can occur is the development of the notion that there is no salvation outside the church. This is because it is easy to classify people in such opposing groups as the faithful and the unfaithful, the good and the evil, saints and sinners—in short, those who are for God and those who are against him. As is often the case when misunderstandings develop, there is some truth involved in the error. The truth here is that the experience of salvation always *results* in membership in the community of the redeemed. The redeemed person never *joins*

112

this community in the same sense in which he may decide to join Trinity Lutheran congregation on Main Street, for he *is* a member by virtue of his relationship to Christ.

The error occurs when the whole thing is turned around and membership in the church is regarded as a condition for achieving salvation instead of the consequence of living in a unique relationship with Christ. The error is compounded when people think of the church simply in terms of historic institutions, such as Roman Catholic, Lutheran, Methodist, Baptist, or any other specialized way of developing patterns of organization. The only criterion John recognized for belonging to the community of the redeemed, the church of Christ, is that the members "have washed their robes and made them white in the blood of the Lamb" (Revelation 7:14). He is equally emphatic in stressing that those who have been redeemed "follow the Lamb wherever he goes" (14:4). The people of God, therefore, are never solitary individuals trudging a lonely road toward eternity. They have learned the deeper meaning of fellowship, and they always welcome and seek the company of others who have known something of the same experience. They are united in a common desire to worship God; they share a common impulse to serve their neighbors in his Name.

But people who are part of the church of Christ are also citizens of the world. They live in civic communities and participate in the affairs that keep the political and economic wheels moving. They have occupations, raise families, watch television, drive cars, and spend their money for things they want. Almost all their daily activities are directly related to the general society of which they are a part. What does John's stress on the serious conflict between the society of men and the community of the redeemed mean for people who realize that they are deeply involved in both?

Retreat from the World

Frequently, Christians have reached the conclusion that they should have nothing to do with the society of men, or at least they should limit their involvement in this society to a minimum. The monastic movement began in the early centuries of the Christian era as a result of a growing conviction that it is impossible to be loyal to Christ while living as a part of general society. At first there were individuals who retreated to isolated spots in the desert or the mountains to spend their lives in prayer and meditation. Later, little communities were formed here and there under the leadership of these hermit monks. Eventually these developed into larger monastic orders with many such communities under a common leadership and a set of common rules.

We should not overlook the fact that these monastic communities often contributed a great deal to the societies within the orbit of their influence. Dedicated monks took care of the sick and helped the needy, and often the monastery was the only place of learning and education in a barbaric environment. But, as a whole, they did not solve the problem of the Christian's relationship to the society of men. It does not take much imagination to realize the chaos that would result if all Christians went off to live in monastic communities. Furthermore, even isolation from society did not save the monks from worldliness. Those who became hermits often discovered that the temptations toward evil increased rather than decreased in their lonely retreats. And the monastic communities, begun with high ideals and subjected to rigid rules of conduct, often became places where high living and even debauchery became customary. The fact is that the Christian cannot escape from the world. Wherever he goes the world goes with him.

Other persons with deep religious sensitivity took a different approach of retreating from the world. There have been quite a few attempts by groups to organize civic communities founded on a special confession of faith. Many of these experiments have taken place in North America. The original Bay State Colony was to some extent such an experiment, and names such as Mormons and Shakers bring to mind other attempts in this direction. But either these experiments slowly died out after the initial enthusiasm had gone, or they gradually became secular communities within the general society.

Domination of Society

Another quite different approach to general society developed in Europe during the Middle Ages. What John describes as Christ's conquest of the nations of the earth (Revelation 19:11–16) was understood by some groups to mean that the church should dominate the society of men. The "doctrine of the two swords," which is the sharpest formulation of this idea, maintains that the head of the church (who, as such, holds the sword of the Word) should also be the supreme authority for the state (and hence also hold the sword of the state). But this approach has resulted not in the Christianizing of secular society but in the secularization of the church. Much the same can be said about the state church system that developed in many Protestant countries after the Reformation.

Social Gospel

In more recent times, especially around the beginning of the twentieth century, there developed yet another outlook, often referred to as the "social gospel" approach. This view, based on a literal interpretation of such New Testament passages as Luke 4:16–21, holds that the chief task of the Christian is to work actively in society for the betterment of living conditions and especially to help those who are oppressed. In doing this, the Christian is carrying out the task of proclaiming the gospel. The social gospel movement was at its peak during the years when there was an optimistic feeling that everything was getting better in the world. Two world wars and continuing tensions on many fronts have eliminated much of that optimism.

Divided Loyalties

Many Christians who can find no solution to the problem of how to relate themselves to the secular world in any of the

REVELATION 20:11–15

approaches discussed above, have drifted into the position that the community of the redeemed and the society of men exist side by side in this world and have little or nothing to do with each other. The result is a sense of divided loyalties and the tacit understanding that church and Sunday go together and that for the rest of the week it is every man for himself.

Can any real guidance in dealing with this problem come from John's book? At first sight it seems as though John has nothing but a blanket condemnation for the society of men. As has been noted before, this society is for him epitomized in the Roman state, and we get the impression that he is rather delighted when "Babylon" finally goes up in smoke. When we recall the moral degeneration and the general corruption of Roman society of John's day, it is not hard to understand this feeling. And there have been other societies since that could match Rome in this respect, just as there have been a number of rulers as vicious as Domitian and Nero. But can we say that all societies are this way?

A little over two hundred years after John wrote his book, a confessed Christian became the ruler of the Roman Empire. Emperor Constantine may not have been a model Christian in all respects, but at least he did not persecute Christians and he did not use the resources of the Roman state to hinder the spread of the gospel. In fact, he did his best to promote Christianity within his realm. What would John have written if he had lived in the fourth century rather than at the end of the first century? And what would he write if he were living in America today?

John's Attitude

At this point it is good to remind ourselves that John is dealing with universal themes in addition to the particular situations which confronted him in his own time.

Keeping this in mind, the first observation to be made is that John did not condemn society itself but a particular kind of society that rebels against God: one in which there is no place for God, in which there is no room for the redemption symbolized by Christ. This kind of society is doomed, says John. It may from time to time show great evidence of strength, but it is the kind of strength that leads to self-destruction. It is the kind of society that will seek to make this world its home, but it will find that this world will not sustain it. It is often a boisterous and self-confident society, but it is also a society in which there is anguish and despair. It is a society in which war and conflict are permanent features and where evil in every form finds fertile soil.

In contrast to this society, John shows the new community of Christians, which may seem to be on the losing side in the conflict between the two but which is, in reality, the source of genuine strength and real hope for the future. The members of this new community acknowledge God as the source and meaning of their existence; they have accepted redemption in Christ as their way of life. They are not a breed of supermen, nor are they immune to the temptations and tribulations in this world; but they do know the source at which human life can be refreshed and renewed.

The New Community

It is in harmony with the interpretation of Revelation that is suggested in this book to say that neither the society of men nor the new community of the redeemed should be identified completely with any historic institution. It is true that the rebellion against God has often come to focus in a secular society such as the Roman Empire in John's day. It is also true that the new community has come to focus in the historic institution of the church. But it would be a mistake to think that the historic church *is* the new community and that secular society *is* the "Babylon" that is doomed. It would be much closer to the truth to say that the struggle between the new community and the society of men is going on in both these institutions, the historic church and secular society.

The church of Laodicea, to all outward appearances a prosperous and successful organization, seemed to have become a part of the society of men. It would not be difficult to point out many other examples in the history of the church where the historic institution seems to have become affiliated with the doomed society of men. And we have no reason to feel confident that this hazard is not a problem in contemporary church life. Likewise, it might be possible to point out instances in which secular society has been the scene of the manifestation of the new community.

Thus the struggle which John describes so vividly in his visions of the future is not a battle between concrete historical institutions but a struggle that takes place in the realm of the spirit. If we acknowledge this, there is no need for us as Christians to feel that we are not able to participate in the affairs of the society in which we are living. But we are obliged to participate as representatives and spokesmen of the new community. This can mean both redemptive wrath and redemptive love or, to use more contemporary terminology, both constructive criticism and positive contribution. However, the fact that we are spokesmen of the new community does not mean that we can regard ourselves as outsiders on temporary duty in an alien environment. The society in which we live is *our* society, and criticism goes hand in hand with acknowledgment of responsibility for the evils that are criticized.

The Doomed Society

What, then, is the doomed society of men that John speaks about? No doubt we can recognize features of this society in the environment in which we live. To use John's language, "Babylon" is not only ancient Rome, it is everywhere, even within the congregation to which we belong. At first thought it may seem odd to associate the picturesque visions of John with the petty and not-so-petty jealousies and conflicts within home, church, and society. But John paints with a large brush. He is enlarging the details of human life and human society to let us see them more clearly. The choice between obedience to God and fellowship with Christ, on the one hand, and rejection of God and redemption, on the other hand, is not a matter of a leisurely, casual choice. There is a life-and-death struggle involving divine and demonic forces in the world, and every moment of our existence we are called to decide where our allegiance is.

Joy

It may seem that life, as pictured here, becomes unbearably serious. Where are the laughter and the fun, the light moments and the casual encounters, the joy of colors and music, the leisure hours and the exciting exploration of places and things? This question is a good one and it needs to be answered, for it is a fact that Christians—at least in some periods—have made life look both unbearably serious and more than a little dull. There have been times when anything beyond a quiet smile was considered frivolous and only the drabbest kind of clothing was thought appropriate to a believer.

Although these views have been unnecessarily extreme, it is well to recognize that there is such a thing as a frivolous approach to life. The person who thinks that "fun" is the common denominator of all worthwhile experiences will not get very far in becoming a real person. Nor is there much depth to any kind of fellowship with other human beings if it is not recognized that there are appropriate serious times.

But one cannot read the Bible without noticing that it expresses a wide kind of response to the delightful and joyous aspects of life. And John's preoccupation with the sounds and sights of his visions does not suggest the tight-lipped pietist whose sensory faculties have become atrophied. It is not difficult to imagine the sound of laughter being heard in the New Jerusalem that John describes in the twenty-first chapter of Revelation. Almost every description of the redeemed throughout his book involves some expression of joy. And it should also be remembered that John does not try to describe every aspect of the Christian's life here on earth. As has been suggested before, he is dealing with certain large themes that are of vital importance in our understanding of life; he is not giving a detailed account of what the Christian must do from cradle to grave.

Perhaps one could best express John's position by saying that there is laughter that expresses the spirit of the new community and there is laughter that reflects hostility toward God. The Christian can have his moments of gaiety and hours of relaxation without thereby deserting his Lord, as long as he doesn't allow his life to become a compulsive quest for enjoyment at any price.

13 · The New Community

THE early Christians were tremendously moved by the new fellowship that their common faith in Christ made available for them. The description of the day of Pentecost (Acts 2), often referred to as the "birthday of the church," reflects this feeling. Reading this and the following chapters in Acts, we get the impression that the church was the center of existence for these first Christians, even to the point where they gave up private property and seemed to live for nothing except "the apostles' teaching and fellowship, . . . the breaking of bread and the prayers" (Acts 2:42). Paul's letters to various congregations also show that he had a genuine love for the fellowship and lived for the purpose of establishing and tending such fellowships wherever he could.

Disruption

The seemingly ideal life of the first church in Jerusalem did not last long. We soon hear of insincerity (Acts 5:1–11) and complaints (Acts 6:1), and Paul often speaks rather sharply in his letters about the faults of church members. Even the leaders of the church had their disagreements and personal differences, and in the letters to the seven churches in the early part of Revelation, only two churches escaped serious criticism. Later, when Constantine made Christianity the state religion of the Roman Empire, there was a great influx of people whose understanding of what it means to be a Christian was slight. In addition, pagan customs and ideas became a part of the teachings and practices of the church.

This process of secularization of the church continued. At the time of the Reformation, things had reached such a point that Luther occasionally referred to the Roman church as "the mother of harlots," the same phrase John had used to describe the society of men run amok. The Reformation undoubtedly purified the church in many ways, but the Protestant churches to which the Reformation gave birth were certainly not perfect, nor are today's denominations ideal examples of the fellowship described in the early chapters of Acts.

As we look back on the history of the church, we can notice that it has had a chameleon-like tendency to absorb local color and adjust to conditions that exist in its society.

The Meaning of the Church

Where, then, is John's new community of the redeemed, the glorious New Jerusalem? This question was asked by some concerned early church fathers, and they wanted to trim the membership rolls of all but the genuine followers of Christ. But this was easier said than done when Christianity became the state religion in the Roman Empire and some of the leading citizens might be among those who should be trimmed. Tertullian, who lived a scant hundred years after John wrote his book, was one of the earliest advocates of this effort to keep the church pure; but only a few people would listen to him, and eventually he broke away from the church and founded a severely ascetic sect of his own.

The view which did take hold was the doctrine that the church is the church of Christ if its leadership is in a direct line of succession from the founding apostles. It would be wrong to say that this completely ignored the criterion that John sets down for membership in the community of the redeemed (Revelation 7:13–14), but it cannot be denied that many ideas and practices were followed that to John would have seemed utterly alien to the meaning of the new community.

Some of the Protestant churches that grew out of the Reformation, especially in the Reformed branch of the Reformation movement, sought to reestablish the principle of a "pure church," or a church in which only genuine followers of Christ are considered members. Some of these have held on to this principle down to the present time. But it has never been an easy principle to put into practice. How can any human being judge the faith or lack of faith in another human being? Often the criteria became external and trivial, such as whether an individual adhered to a narrowly conceived code of conduct.

Luther, who said that the true church is to be found wherever the Word is rightly preached and the sacraments are rightly administered, avoided these pitfalls. But even this did not make the church safe from secularization. In the latter part of the seventeenth century the Pietist movement developed as a protest against the formalism and intellectualism of the Lutheran church. It attempted to identify the new community of the redeemed as the "church within the church," the little group of devout Christians within a larger congregation. In its best period Pietism was a strong power in European church life, inspiring foreign missions and social work as well as Bible study and personal devotion. But eventually it came to be almost synonymous with narrowness and emotionalism, so that today the name itself has a rather derogatory connotation.

A Place of Friendship?

Confronted with this history of thought about the meaning of the church, the modern Christian may well wonder if he has any chance of coming to terms with the meaning of the church. He is apt to simply conclude that the church is the church because it bears the name of a church. He may feel vaguely that his church is in some way better than other churches, although he cannot help noticing that his neighbor feels the same way about his own church. He knows that there are certain duties and responsibilities that go with church membership: giving money, being "active" in one way or another, fairly regular attendance at worship, living a decent life, and getting along with his fellow church members.

But does this add up to what John calls the New Jerusalem, the holy city that has all the beauty and excitement of a bride getting ready to meet her husband? Does the average modern church member's heart beat a little faster in anticipation as he prepares to attend church on Sunday morning? If he were pressed to state just what experience as a church member has meant the most to him, perhaps he would say the friendly association with other people like himself, both at worship and in other church activities. This may be so for people who have had a lifelong association with the same congregation. And it may be even more true for those who have had to move from place to place often, for they find that the church is often the quickest way to form new associations and friendships in a strange community. For parents who have growing children the church is a great boon, for they feel assured that there their sons and daughters will meet "other nice young people" and become interested in "wholesome activities."

An "In-Group"

This quite general appreciation of the fellowship which can be enjoyed through membership in a church may serve as a springboard for some more thought about the new community that we find pictured in Revelation. To do so we shall first consider a term that is often used by sociologists in their discussion of human associations, the "in-group." The in-group is a natural affiliation of people who are sufficiently alike in their ideas, tastes, way of living, and other characteristics, to feel at ease and happy in each other's company. An outsider who differs significantly from the members of the in-group will not do very well in such a group: he will feel uncomfortable, and so will the members. In some cases they will try to tolerate him, but often they will make it quite clear that he is not welcome. The only way in which someone can be fully accepted into an in-group is by his possessing the characteristics that hold the in-group members together. If he does not, he is in some way unworthy of the fellowship.

The purpose of this discussion of the sociologist's in-group concept is to suggest that much modern church life seems to be an in-group experience. Those who gather together under the same church roof are people who are enough alike to enjoy each other's company. They meet and greet each other with the comfortable feeling that they are among their peers, and they get no little support from the thought that there are so many others who live the same way they do. The phrase that is often displayed on bulletin boards and church stationery, "The Friendly Church," may well mean this: "Those who are like us will find a friendly reception here."

The Modern Heresy

The developments in recent years relating to racial segregation and inner-city church work have thrown a strong light on the in-group character of much modern church life. The fact that many churches and church leaders have been reluctant to eliminate racial barriers, and the even more baffling fact that some church people have been actively opposed to integration despite the clear message of the Bible in this regard, point clearly to the in-group feeling as a major obstacle. It is not uncommon to see a large and gracious old church, located in what has become a slum neighborhood, maintained by a handful of members while the surrounding streets are teeming with people who do not feel welcome inside the walls of this exclusive building.

This confusion of the in-group with the new community as the essential meaning of the church may not be a strictly modern phenomenon, but it seems so widespread in contemporary church life that one could call it the "great modern heresy." As is the case with all heresies, there is some truth in the error. The truth here is the fact that church life does imply fellowship. This is given emphatic expression in the statement from the Book of Acts that "the company of those who believed were of one heart and soul" (4:32). We must also recognize that everyone needs some form of in-group fellowship if he is not to feel like a total stranger in this world. The heresy is neither the in-group experience as such nor the strong feeling of fellowship within the church, but the confusion of the two.

Basis of Fellowship

How, then, does the new community in Revelation differ from the in-group? The first thing to be noted is that the *basis* for the fellowship is different. We become members of an in-group because we possess certain characteristics that, in the eyes of other members, make us worthy of the fellowship. In in-groups inspired largely by hate and prejudice, these qualities are highly regarded, although they may not seem very worthy to an outsider. In the new community, on the other hand, what brings people together is their complete lack of worthiness. They have no qualities that make them acceptable. The in-group member will ask, openly or unconsciously "Is he as good as I am?" The member of the new community will say, "I am as bad as he is!" And this is not merely a play on words, for it points to two fundamentally different reasons for accepting another person as one's equal.

The in-group member will always find people that he cannot accept into his fellowship, and he will also find that there are those who will not accept him. But the member of the new community will have no reason for excluding anyone. He is not any better than anyone else, and for this reason he can accept everyone as a potential brother or sister. The "dividing wall" of which Paul spoke has been broken down, and a true community can be established, one in which there is "no distinction" (Romans 3:22b–23) based on the achievements or attributes of individuals. The new community is an open community, as is beautifully indicated in John's statement that the gates of the New Jerusalem are never shut (Revelation 21:25). Anyone and everyone belongs here.

This description of the new community will no doubt raise some questions. Does not this notion of fellowship run counter to every natural human instinct? Does not the idea that "I am no better than he is" destroy every vestige of self-respect? Does not the open character of the new community destroy every standard and tradition? Is not the whole idea a hopelessly impractical theory in the world in which we are living?

Nature of the New Community

These questions, and many similar ones that could be added, help to point out the difference between any kind of natural association of men and the new community. John makes his point quite clear: the New Jerusalem he saw was "coming down out of heaven from God" (21:2), and its appearance was accompanied by the statement "Behold, I make all things new" (21:5). The new community is not a natural association but emerges as something that is utterly novel and unprecedented. There is no way in which we can explain the meaning of the new community by reference to what we experience and learn simply as citizens of this world.

What, then, is the nature of this new community? First of all, it is a community that owes its existence entirely to Christ and his redemptive work. We may organize local congregations, but we never organize the new community. We may elect church leaders, but Christ is the only head of the new community. Our churches and denominations may grow old and stale, but the new community is always fresh and delightful as a "bride adorned for her husband" (21:2). We expend money and labor to keep our congregations and denominations going and progressing, and we should and must do this; but the new community is an absolutely free gift. We keep records of church members, often dividing them up into a number of categories; but the only record of the members of the new community is "written in the Lamb's book of life" (21:27).

Second, we can enter this community only in response to an invitation. This is made clear in the old Greek word used

REVELATION 21:9–10

to describe the church, *ekklesia* (from *ek,* meaning "out"; and *kalein,* meaning "to call"). The members of the new community are there because they have been called or invited. But the only one who can issue this invitation is Christ. When we invite people through the preaching of the Word and in other ways, it is only as his spokesmen and with no authority of our own.

We plainly have no right, then, no authority, to refuse fellowship with anyone who has responded to the call of Christ. Any kind of racial or social discrimination in church life is a radical denial of Christ and his new community. If we want our churches to be manifestations of the new community, there can be no justification for keeping away anyone who has heard the call of Christ and responded to it. Have we no right to refuse membership under any circumstance? John speaks of some who cannot enter the open gates of the New Jerusalem: "Nothing unclean shall enter it, nor any one who practices abomination or falsehood . . ." (21:27). But John's language here makes it clear that these are people who reject Christ and his redeeming work. They are invited but they refuse the invitation, just like the people Christ spoke about in the Parable of the Banquet (Luke 14:15–24; cf. Revelation 19:9). In the New Testament there are warnings against the danger of false teachers as well as church members who in word and deed deny the meaning of the redemption in Christ. Paul cautions believers not to be "mismated with unbelievers" (2 Corinthians 6:14). But we have to be very sure that we are using the right criterion when we are making judgments of this nature. In particular, the racial and national origin of a person, his social and economic status, his education, and even his habits of personal cleanliness, have nothing to do with whether he is acceptable in the church that desires to be a manifestation of the new community. And even when we ask questions concerning his faith and behavior, we must be sure that we are not letting our own limited perspective obscure the real criterion—whether he is responding to the call from Christ. We would do well here in remembering how Jesus often scandalized the more respectable people in his day by his generous acceptance of all kinds of people.

Need for Organization

The distinction between the church as a cultural and historical institution and the new community has sometimes led people to conclude that there is no need to bother with any form of organized church life. Why cannot one simply be a member of the new community without getting entangled in the complex and often frustrating details of a church organization?

People who think this way have not fully understood the meaning of the new community. It is in the nature of this new community that it seeks to become manifest in human life, in cultural and historical institutions. We cannot take for granted that the new community is always manifest in a congregation simply because it is called a church. Nor can we assume that everything done in the name of a church is necessarily the work of God. The examples of the churches of Sardis and Laodicea serve as warnings here.

But where should one look for the manifestation of the new community if not where people gather to worship, to hear the Word, and to celebrate the sacraments? Furthermore, the new community is not just a fellowship of the individual believer with Christ. It is a triangular fellowship relating the individual both to Christ and to other human beings. This fellowship is not limited to activities in the church or to members of the church. But where can one learn to practice this fellowship if not in the church? It would take a very rare kind of person to live under the terms of the new community without being drawn to some group of people who are likewise engaged.

Imperfections

What, then, about the many imperfections in our local church, the tensions and trivialities and monotony that kill enthusiasm and deaden the sense of expectancy? Here we should remember that one of the chief functions of church life is repentance—as John points out in his messages to the seven churches. This means individual repentance for personal faults, but it also means group repentance for letting the organized institution obscure the meaning of the new community. When we read the words of the confession, "We have sinned against thee by thought, word, and deed," we usually apply this to ourselves as individuals. New life could be felt in our church if we could also learn to say this as a group.

Ecumenicity

The distinction between the church as a cultural and historic institution and the new community may also shed some light on the problem of our relationship to other denominations and confessions. The fact that the Christian church is divided into so many separate organizations may be a scandal, as some people say. But the new community is never divided. It may be a good thing for separated Christians to get together; many of the reasons that have kept them apart are hardly valid. But insofar as they are members of the new community they are already united, and nothing should prevent Christians from extending the hand of fellowship wherever they find some sign of the new community. To let forms of worship, or even formal creedal statements, stand in the way here is to let the institution obscure the meaning of the new community.

The appearance of the new community is on all occasions a joyful event, and we should say that it is also an eternally contemporary event. There is nothing in all of life that can compare with the experience of fellowship according to the terms of the new community. This is no doubt why John's description of the New Jerusalem in the twenty-first chapter is so vivid. And it may not be too much to say that it is some intimation of the possibilities of this new community, however dimly these may be perceived, that gives meaning to all human existence.

14 · History and the New Community

FOR some people, history is mainly a dull recital of old dates and names far removed from the excitement of present-day living. But history can and should be a fascinating drama that is relevant to life now. What makes history come alive is the discovery that actions pertain to real people who were faced with important choices and, in making them, helped to shape the developments that have led to our own way of life. Equally important is the realization that history is not just something that happened in the past but is constantly being made, and that we are now doing things that future generations will look back upon with either appreciation or regret.

Change

One undeniable characteristic of history is change. Changes may occur slowly or rapidly. They may be orderly or revolutionary, but they are always taking place. Some people welcome change and try to speed the process. Others are afraid of change and try to stem the rising tide. Most of us have something of both attitudes within us, and for this reason we are both apprehensive and hopeful when we turn our faces toward the future.

Why do changes occur? The general answer to this question is that all life undergoes change. The basic processes of birth, growth, development, and ultimate decay are forms of change. We love babies, but we would be worried if they remained in an infantile state for a long period of time. There seems to be in all life an irresistible drive toward fulfillment, a constant moving forward which means, at the same time, that something is left behind. If we want to become adults, we must be prepared to give up the security of our childhood.

Birth and Death

Many students of history have been convinced that there is a close parallel between the changes that take place in human life from cradle to grave and the long-range historical changes that can be observed. Nations and cultures emerge and grow great, but then they decay and disappear. In the days of Moses and the Exodus, for instance, Pharaoh and his war chariots were a formidable threat to the people of Israel; but they did not present any problem at the time John was writing his book. The ruthless Babylonians who had destroyed Jerusalem and razed the Temple in the sixth century before Christ had long since ceased to be a menace, too. And even the Roman Empire that John saw as the epitome of evil and opposition to Christ and his church came to an end more than a thousand years ago. If we project this pattern into the future, it means that the nations and cultures we know now will disappear and be replaced.

If we look at history this way, we may easily come to the conclusion that it is just a series of repetitions. The changes that take place seem to be merely like the revolutions of a gigantic wheel turning with a kind of inevitable and impersonal precision as the centuries pass by. But the voice from Revelation sounds a different note: "Behold, I make all things new" (21:5). There is more to life than a tedious repetition of what has happened in the past.

134

Attraction of the New

What is the magic attraction of the word "new"? A child will respond with joy when he is given a new toy or a new article of clothing. As adults we may curb our outward expressions, but there is no denying that we are fascinated by what is new and spend both time and effort in its pursuit. Modern advertisers, realizing this, stress the element of newness in almost all their products, from soap powders to clothing to automobiles. Our economy depends heavily on the idea that people will buy new things long before the old things have ceased to be useful.

The pursuit of the new in the form of material things may be something peculiar to modern Western civilization, but the quest for the new is not. The very old myth of the phoenix, the bird that burned to death but rose again from the ashes with new life, expresses a universal human desire. This myth, which can be found in some form in all parts of the world, points to what is really the motive in the quest for the new: the desire for the renewal of life. A beautiful expression of this desire is found in the Book of Isaiah, which speaks of those who "shall renew their strength, they shall mount up with wings like eagles, they shall run and not be weary, they shall walk and not faint" (40:31).

The desire for the new or for the renewal of life implies that the old has not been fully satisfying. The young person looks toward adult life with anticipation, dreaming of the fine and exciting things he will do when he comes into his own. But more often than not he finds himself drawn into a humdrum and disappointing existence where his high sense of expectation is gradually pared down. The young people who marry with the conviction that their love for each other is strong enough to provide a lifetime of romantic fulfillment may find themselves looking at each other with calculating and critical eyes. An eloquent testimony to the disillusionments of life is the automobile graveyard where the cars that just a few years ago were advertised as the greatest engineering achievements in the world are rusting and falling apart.

Facing Disillusionment

What can we do when we are faced with these disillusionments? We can try something new, hoping it will be better. And it is really amazing how persistently we continue to do this in spite of one disillusionment after another. The frustrated drudge will think about getting a new job or dream about the big break that will make everything right. After delivering our old car to the junkyard we will take our money happily to a new-car dealer and proudly contemplate all the "new" features that we can enjoy in the newer model. The partners from a broken marriage go looking for new romance.

No matter how much life has disappointed us, we are reluctant to give up the hope that something will yet emerge. Sometimes if we are finally forced to relinquish this hope there seems to be little reason to go on living.

This interaction of disappointment and the quest for renewal is not just characteristic of individual human lives but seems to run through all history. Every historical change is a movement away from a form of life that is no longer satisfactory and toward a "better" way. The American Revolution is a good example here. The colonial status, "taxation without representation," was no longer adequate for the rapidly growing culture on the western side of the Atlantic; and independent self-government seemed far better. The Communist is also convinced that his way of life is far better than anything that has been practiced in the past. Alexander the Great, one of the first would-be conquerors of the whole world, thought he was doing the world a favor by subjecting nations to the influence of Hellenic culture even if he achieved this by the power of the sword.

However, it is clear that not everything new has the power to effect a genuine renewal of life. In fact, the quest for the new often merely sets the stage for new disappointments. This is the point of John's description of the fall of Babylon (Revelation 18). Babylon, or the society of men, had promised so many things: sensual enjoyment, all the good things that money can buy, music and all the arts. To those who were committed to Babylon she looked like a splendorous and satisfying answer to the human quest for the renewal of life. The "great city that was clothed in fine linen, in purple and scarlet, bedecked with gold, with jewels, and with pearls" (18:16) was a real competitor to the New Jerusalem. It is no wonder that those who loved her were "weeping and mourning aloud" as they saw her going up in smoke.

The Human Tragedy

According to John, the human tragedy both in our individual lives and in the flow of historical events is that the quest for the renewal of life is directed toward things that cannot bring about this renewal. The only genuine renewal of life comes to those who "have washed their robes and made them white in the blood of the Lamb" (Revelation 7:14), who have come to know the meaning of redemption and life as it is understood in terms of the new community. The new community is therefore the answer to all the questions man can ask concerning the meaning of his historical existence. The fulfillment of man's historical existence is in the new community.

Does this mean that, in spite of the many signs to the contrary, the history of man is moving toward a day when, as the old prophet put it, "the earth will be filled with the knowledge of the glory of the LORD, as the waters cover the sea" (Habbakkuk 2:14)? And how does all this affect the Christian's attitude toward the world in which he lives?

If every human heart is in some way searching for the renewal of life, how are we to understand John when he speaks about those who are excluded from the New Jerusalem, the "dogs and sorcerers and fornicators and murderers and idolaters, and every one who loves and practices falsehood" (Revelation 22:15)? We can say that these vices represent a denial of the spirit of the new community, and that so long as this denial persists, the search for the renewal of life will be in vain. But he who knows that it took a miracle of grace to show him the way, and that he must be sustained daily by

137

this same grace, will not be quick to judge others. He will look, rather, for signs of grace doing its work even in the most unlikely places. And he will meet every human being with the awareness that they share his concern for the renewal of life, no matter how much they differ in other respects.

Pessimism Versus Optimism

It is true that Christians have often thought that there were evil people in this world who justly deserved to be damned. Moreover, they have thought that these people comprised the majority of the world's population and that it is wrong to hope for a better world until God destroys all evildoers. That John's book has often been interpreted in this way cannot be denied. The misinterpretations apply to certain statements by Christ in the Gospels and to other portions of the Bible.

One of the aims of this study has been to show that such an interpretation rests on a misunderstanding of the methods and purpose of apocalyptic literature. And, furthermore, such an interpretation is highly inconsistent with the basic teachings of the Bible. What does the missionary command to "make disciples of all nations" (Matthew 28:19) mean, if not that the new community will make its effect felt throughout the world? Are the words of the Lord's Prayer, "Thy kingdom come, thy will be done, on earth as it is in heaven," merely an empty gesture? On the contrary, they are revolutionary petitions designed to turn much of our current community values completely upside down, if we mean what we pray.

Could it be that the pessimistic view of the destruction of the world becomes an excuse for not doing what we are called to do? It is much easier to just wait for the return of Christ, like the servant who buried his talent in the ground waited for the return of his master, than to become involved in the affairs of the world as a Christian. Are we like Jonah, who sat outside Nineveh hopefully waiting for the destruction of the city, who was displeased when the citizens repented and the fireworks did not appear?

138

Revelation 22:10–12

Turning to God

It is true that John's book contains a clear warning against basing our hopes for the future on the natural developments of the society of men. But at the same time he envisions a "new heaven and a new earth" (Revelation 21:1) where the New Jerusalem occupies a central position. This vision has been interpreted to mean a radical re-creation of the whole universe at some future time, but the language used here suggests that John is speaking in symbolic terms, just as he spoke in symbolic terms concerning the natural disasters of the trumpets and the bowls. His point is this: where the new community becomes manifest, nature itself will sustain and comfort man instead of making him insecure and fearful. Redemption does not involve just the relationship of man and God, but as Paul also hints (Romans 8:19–25), man's relationship to nature.

John's visions of the future thus point to the possibility of a day when the human race will turn to God and worship him and the new community will be the dominant pattern of fellowship among men. It would be foolish to speculate on when this day will come, but it can be a powerful inspiration for the Christian as he dedicates his life and abilities to the task of helping to hasten its coming.

How does this view differ, then, from the evolutionary view of history discussed earlier? Both views look forward to a better future. But there is a difference of radical importance. The evolutionary view takes for granted that the better future will emerge as the society of men gradually improves. John's vision, on the other hand, is based on the needed manifestation of the new community of the redeemed, both now and in the future, standing as a judgment upon the society of men.

Life in the New Jerusalem

In John's description of the New Jerusalem, he says that he "saw no temple in the city, for its temple is the Lord God the Almighty and the Lamb" (21:22). This is to say that in the new world there will be no need for special places of worship and for what we conventionally call "religion." Life itself will be worship and "religion" will be the doing of one's daily task. The familiar distinction between the sacred and the world will disappear, and the world will no longer be a temptation and a stumbling block.

Phrases like "the water of life," "the tree of life," and "the healing of the nations" (22:1–5) also point to the quality of life that will be possible in the new world. The quest for the renewal of life will no longer take odd and devious forms but will lead man to the true source of life in the new community of the redeemed.

As we contemplate the meaning of John's New Jerusalem and the new world of his vision, we might find it difficult to connect this picture with the world in which we are living now. It would seem much simpler to say that John is describing heaven in this final vision, and that this is the kind of existence we may hope for after death. Furthermore, even if John's vision describes some state of being here on earth, it must be in a future so distant that we who are living now will not have the slightest chance of experiencing it. Here, once more, it will be well to remember that the purpose of John's visions of the future is not to describe a world of the future only, but to call attention to the possibilities of living creatively and effectively in our world now. In a very real sense all that John speaks about, both the disintegration of the society of men and the manifestation of the new community, are events that are taking place now. Every day of the Christian's life can be a reliving of the drama of Revelation. And in this way of living there is both hope for the future and a clear call to action.

Then I saw a new Heaven and a new earth, for the first Heaven and the first earth had disappeared, and the sea was no more. I saw the holy city, the new Jerusalem, descending from God out of Heaven, prepared as a bride dressed in beauty for her husband. Then I heard a great voice from the throne crying:

"See! The home of God is with men, and he will live among them. They shall be his people, and God himself shall be with them, and will wipe away every tear from their eyes. Death shall be no more, and never again shall there be sorrow or crying or pain. For all those former things are past and gone."

Then he who is seated upon the throne said, "See, I am making all things new!"

And he added,

"Write this down, for my words are true and to be trusted."

Then he said to me:

"It is done! I am Alpha and Omega, the beginning and the end. I will give to the thirsty water without price from the fountain of life. The victorious shall inherit these things, and I will be God to him and he will be son to me."

REVELATION 21:1–7
J. B. Phillips translation